The Murder of Rebecca Schaeffer & Other Stories

Samantha Reeder

Published by Richard Poche, 2021.

THE MURDER OF REBECCA SCHAEFFER & OTHER STORIES

First edition. July 9, 2021.

Copyright © 2021 Samantha Reeder.

ISBN: 979-8224751709

Written by Samantha Reeder.

THE MURDER OF REBECCA SCHAEFFER & OTHER STORIES

SAMANTHA REEDER

Murder is tragic no matter when it happens, but society has a stronger reaction to murder when it happens to someone who is loved and adored by all, someone famous, someone for whom life has been cut too short. When an actress is murdered, when her potential for future success taken away, the world seems to stop for a moment. And in the case of Rebecca Schaeffer, everyone is still asking why.

Her friends and family were robbed of years of her life. Her fans were robbed of hours of entertainment that she seemed destined for.

The Beginning

Rebecca Lucile Schaeffer was born November 6, 1967 to a Jewish family in Eugene, Oregon. She was the only child of Danna, a writer and teacher at the local college, and Dr. Benson Schaeffer, a child psychologist. Rebecca thought about becoming a rabbi but fate would intervene during her teen years.

Rebecca began modeling in her junior year of high school. She appeared in catalogs for department stores, television commercials, and was even an extra in a television film. She appeared to have found her calling and her parents were supportive of it.

In 1984, they allowed her to move to New York City to continue pursuing her a possible career in modeling and acting. While in New York, she attended the Professional Children's School, a school dedicated to educating young actors and dancers.

A Budding Career

In the later half of 1984, Rebecca won the role of Annie Barnes on ABC's *One Life to Live*, a soap opera. She would occupy that role for six months. In that time, she attempted to continue pursuing her modeling prospects, but it did not look good for her. Standing at 5'7", she was considered too short for high fashion modeling and therefore struggled to find work.

As a result of this, Rebecca decided to move to Japan in hopes of finding modeling jobs despite her height. But the results were no different in Tokyo than they were in New York. So, reluctantly, she returned to New York City and decided that acting was the way to go. She ceased her pursuit of modeling and dedicated her time and energy to her acting career.

By 1986, after two years of struggling to find her purpose, Rebecca had landed herself a small role in Woody Allen's comedy *Radio Days*. Unfortunately, her performance was edited out of the film before it reached production. Only a brief scene featuring her character, with no lines, remains in the film.

While working on her acting career, Rebecca still found the need to pick up modeling contracts and work as a waitress in order to survive. After landing the cover of *Seventeen* magazine, Rebecca caught the attention of television producers who were working on a new sitcom. This sitcom was called *My Sister Sam*, and would star Pam Dawber of *Mork and Mindy* fame.

Rebecca auditioned for the role of Patricia "Patti" Russell, a teenager who moved from Oregon to San Francisco to live with her 29-year-old sister, Samantha "Sam" Russell, after the death of their parents. Rebecca won the role and was set to take on her first major part in any film production.

The sitcom was a hit, initially. It rated in the top 25 shows on television. However, halfway through the second season, in April 1988, it was cancelled due to low ratings. Fans petitioned to have it continue, but ultimately the studio cancelled it.

Following her appearance in *My Sister Sam*, Rebecca landed supporting roles in *Scenes from the Class Struggle in Beverly Hills*, *The End of Innocence*, and *Out of Time*, a television film. She also worked as a spokesperson for the children's charity, Thursday's Child.

The future looked bright for Rebecca Schaeffer. For someone so young, she was starting to build a solid foundation of acting and modeling roles that would pave the way for a successful future in the industry. However, that future was never to come to fruition.

The Murderer

Robert John Bardo was born in 1983 and grew up in Tuscon, Arizona. His mother was Korean and his father was a non-commissioned officer in the U.S. Air Force. He had a troubled childhood, being mentally and physically abused by one of his siblings. He was placed into foster care after he threatened to commit suicide because of the continual abuse. One of his teachers described him as a "ticking time bomb" and her words would prove to be prophetic.

The Bardo family had a history of mental health issues and Robert was no exception having been diagnosed with manic depression at a young age. At 15, he was institutionalized for a month due to his emotional problems. He dropped out of high school in the ninth grade, for reasons unknown, and began working as a janitor at a Jack in the Box.

In the eighteen months prior to the murder of Rebecca Schaeffer, Bardo was arrested three times on charges of domestic violence and disorderly conduct. Neighbors of the young man indicated that he often exhibited strange and unexplainable behavior. He would threaten one neighbor more than once while physically assaulting another.

Robert developed an obsession with famous people in his teenage years and it extended into his young adult years. Robert was obsessed with Samantha Smith, a child peace activist. Smith would die tragically in a plane crash in 1985 and Bardo needed another celebrity to obsess on.

He found her in Rebecca Schaeffer.

He wrote numerous letters to Rebecca over the next three years. One of her fan services representatives even responded to him and sent him an autograph. In 1987, he traveled to Los Angeles to meet Schaeffer on the set of *My Sister Sam*, but was turned away by Warner Bros security.

Angered by this rejection, he returned a month later with a knife but was once again turned away by security. Defeated, Robert returned to Tucson and began letter writing campaigns to other celebrities such as Debbie Gibson, Madonna and Tiffany.

But in 1989, Robert Bardo saw Rebecca in *Scenes from the Class Struggle in Beverly Hills*. In the black comedy, Rebecca's character appeared in bed with a fellow male actor. This scene was enough to throw Robert into a jealous rage. It made him angry at Rebecca for simply becoming "another Hollywood whore".

Robert set to work deciding on how to enact his revenge. He learned of a man who had stalked and stabbed actress Theresa Saldana in 1982. Arthur Richard Jackson had used a private investigator in order to obtain Theresa Saldana's home address. Encouraged by this success, Robert sought out to do the same.

He paid $250 to a detective agency in Tucson to obtain Rebecca's address from the California Department of Motor Vehicle's records. With her street address in hand, he then turned to his brother to get a gun. Robert was only nineteen and could not legally buy a gun in Arizona but his older brother was able to give him a .357 caliber Ruger handgun.

Now with address and gun in hand, Bardo set off for Los Angeles.

After locating Rebecca's neighborhood, he spent some time asking around to be sure that she lived there. Her neighbors were less than helpful in confirming her location. Robert Bardo decided that it was best to simply take matters into his own hands. He approached what he believed to be her apartment building and rang the buzzer. And on that day Robert Bardo would make history. His actions and his name would not be forgotten any time soon.

The Murder

On July 18, 1989, Rebecca Schaeffer was home preparing to audition for a role in *The Godfather Part III*. That was when she heard someone buzz at the door of her Los Angeles apartment. Expecting the delivery of a film script, Rebecca didn't hesitate to go down to the front entrance of her apartment building in order to sign for it with the courier.

Instead, when Rebecca opened the door she came face-to-face with Robert John Bardo who introduced himself as a big fan of Rebecca's work. He even presented her with a letter and autograph that he believed she had sent him. They initially had a friendly exchange, but after a few moments, Rebecca asked him to leave so she can get back to rehearsing. She also asked him to never visit her at home again. Robert obliged and left the apartment to go to a local coffee shop.

While at the coffee shop, Robert John Bardo took out a gun, loaded it, and then returned to Rebecca's apartment building an hour later. Rebecca heard another buzz at the door and made her way downstairs a second time. Hoping that this time it is actually the courier at the door with her script.

However, when she got to the front door of the building, she was surprised that it was once again Robert Bardo who was at the door. She had "a cold look on her face" Bard later said. She told him that she was busy and again asked him to leave.

Robert Bardo did not take rejection a second time very well. He reached into a paper bag he was holding and pulled out the gun that he had loaded at the coffee shop. He pointed it at Rebecca and fired off a single shot to her chest at point blank range.

Rebecca crashed to the ground, screaming. Robert Bardo fled the scene. When the paramedics arrived at the scene, Rebecca was still breathing. She was quickly loaded into an ambulance and rushed to the hospital in the hope that they could save her life. Unfortunately, about a half-hour later she was pronounced dead at Cedars-Sinai Medical Center.

Rebecca Schaeffer was not known to have any enemies so immediately friends and family begin to believe that the suspect in this case must be a deranged fan. There could be no one else responsible for the attack. Nothing else made sense.

A day after her murder, police found Robert Bardo in Tucson, Arizona. There were various reports of a man running through traffic on Interstate 10, which led the police to him. Robert Bardo immediately confessed at the scene. "You better arrest me now. I shot somebody."

Bardo was charged with first-degree murder. His public defender stated that Robert Bardo takes daily medication for a mental illness, but indicated that he is of sound mind to continue with a trial. And as such, he proceeded to stand trial for what he'd done.

Sentencing

In 1991, Robert John Bardo was convicted of capital murder in a bench trial. He agreed to be tried by a judge alone without a jury present. It was not a matter of if Bardo had committed the crime. Everyone knew that he was guilty. It was a matter of why he had committed the crime. During the trial, Bardo was housed in the Sensitive Needs Unit, which was reserved for gang members, notorious prisoners, and those convicted of sex crimes. The court wanted to ensure that nothing happened to him before a verdict could be reached.

Prosecutor Marcia Clark, Deputy District Attorney, worked the trial. She would later become famous for her role in the O. J. Simpson case, but was a reputable prosecutor in her own right at the time of this trial. Clark maintained that this was a premeditated murder as Robert Bardo had tried to meet Rebecca Schaeffer on multiple occasions. He acquired her address. He acquired a gun. It was clear that he planned the event. And Clark pushed to state that Robert Bardo was not mentally ill, that he was sound of mind enough to plan out the events of the case.

Robert Bardo's lawyer brought forward expert testimony that Bardo suffered from schizophrenia and that he could not distinguish between right and wrong. Psychiatrist Park Dietz testified to that fact. And that, despite acquiring the gun and the address, he did not decide to kill Rebecca Schaeffer until moments before he shot her in the chest. It was not premeditated but rather an impulsive act of violence.

The prosecution called to the stand a Warner Bros security guard. The guard told the court that he turned Robert Bardo away when the obsessive fan attempted to visit Rebecca at the studio. It was a fairly common thing to do. The security guard described Robert Bardo as "calm, rational, and intelligent" when they had encountered each other. He indicated that there was nothing unstable about the man.

Robert Bardo's lawyer continued to push the insanity defense. In order to do that, he introduced a jailhouse interview that was conducted two days before the trial began. This video became crucial to the defense. In it, Bardo stated that he almost had a heart attack upon learning that Schaeffer was dead from the television and that, after shooting her, he almost turned the gun on himself.

"It was a weird idea to know that I had killed somebody," Robert stated in the interview with Dr. Park Dietz. And as he listened to the account of the event during the trial, Bardo hung his head and pressed his fists to his ears. He seemed very much in denial about the fact that what he'd done was actually reality.

Bardo went on to state that when he'd gone to her door a second time "she was in her bathrobe and I was thinking this is the wrong time. She's taking a shower." He continued in his recollection and stated, "she said: 'you came to my door again.' And it was like I was bothering her again. 'Hurry up, I don't have much time.'"

"I thought that was a very callous thing to say to a fan," Bardo said, adding that it was then he shot her.

"She was just screaming," Barrdo said, going as far as to imitate her cries. "She was going: 'Why? Why?' I was still fumbling around, thinking I should blow my head off and fall on her".

In the tape Bardo also talked about his interest in other obsessed fans who attacked performers. He had followed the story of Arthur Jackson's attack on Theresa Saldana. He had visited the spot where

Mark David Chapman killed John Lennon while he was trying to meet Debbie Gibson, who he had also been stalking, in New York.

The defense worked hard to blame the incident on mental illness and went as far as to blame a song for inciting Robert's violence. Bardo had sat stone-faced through most of his trial until a song by U2 called "Exit" was played as part of the defense. When the song was played, Bardo began mouthing the lyrics and rocking back and forth. According to the defense, the song played a large role in spurring on his murder of Rebecca Schaeffer.

After a month of testimony, the judge rendered the verdict of guilty in the charge of first-degree murder. In December of 1991, Robert John Bardo was sentenced to life in prison without the possibility of parole. He is currently serving this sentence at the Ironwood State Prison in Riverside County, California.

Still, two decades after the murder of Rebecca Schaeffer, legal experts continue to debate the same thing: does Robert Bardo's mental illness rise to the level of legal insanity? For the most part, legal scholars agree that he does not have a substantial case for legal insanity.

Changes to the Law

Following what had happened to Theresa Saldana and Rebecca Schaeffer, California was forced to re-evaluate its laws in relation to personal information. These two incidents resulted in drastic changes to the policies and practices around a person's information and who has access to it.

In 1989, Los Angeles Police created the nation's first team dedicated to and specializing in stalking investigations. In 1994, California passed the Driver's Privacy Protection Act. This act would prevent the Department of Motor Vehicles from releasing the private addresses of license holders.

Additionally, when Rebecca Schaeffer was alive, no states in the United States of America had anti-stalking laws. In five short years after her death, all fifty states had enacted anti-stalking laws. The first state to do this was California in 1990. The laws were geared to protect the victims of stalkers.

An Unattained Future

Following her death, Rebecca was seen alongside Burt Lancaster and Eva Marie Saint in *Voyage of Terror: The Achille Lauro Affair*. It was reported that, had she not died, Rebecca Schaeffer may have played the role of Vivian Ward in *Pretty Woman*, a part which was given to Julia Roberts in 1990.

On the day that Rebecca died, she was scheduled to meet with Francis Ford Coppola about a role in *The Godfather Part III*. She was reportedly waiting for a courier to deliver the script when she opened the door to her murderer.

Rebecca Schaeffer was on the road to a bright future, a future that was cut short by a crazed stalker. Hollywood may have been a different place had Rebecca Schaeffer continued to score roles on the big screen. Icons may have changed; careers may have never taken off. It is a fact that we will never be able prove, but Rebecca was stolen from the world and it will never be forgotten.

A Mother's Message

In order to cope with her daughter's death, Rebecca's mother Danna Schaeffer, wrote and preformed a one woman show titled *You in Midair*. In her performance, Danna provides the audience with a vivid retelling of the painful ordeal of losing her daughter. She tells her audience about getting the news, flying to Los Angeles, and having to visit the morgue to identify the body. She tells of the trial and what it did to her and her marriage. She tells the audience of her experience with therapy in order to cope with the ordeal.

The performance, meant to help Danna cope, took its toll on her husband who was not quite as liberated by the event. Still, she continues to perform, as it is what she needs to do to handle the loss of her only child, to try to make sense of what happened despite the senselessness of the event.

"Part of me always felt like I'm not going to let life do this to me," Danna said. "I'm not going to take it lying down. Maybe I physically wanted to show people, hey, here we are. We're all right... I couldn't second-guess myself and I couldn't tailor [my story] to be what somebody else thought a grieving mother should be like or what good theater should be like or what would be acceptable to anybody. I just had to cut loose and cutting loose to me was not editing things out."

She went on to offer a message to all parents. "I see parents who are disappointed in their [children] because they have expectations that the kids can't live up to," she said. "And I guess if they were to take something it would be to just admire their children for who they are and tell them so. Rebecca had the passion, energy and courage to pursue her talent."

Danna is currently regrouping but dreams of doing another run of *You in Midair* in Los Angeles, in the Prague Fringe Festival, and in Paris.

In Conclusion

The obsessive devotion of one man resulted in the death of a rising star. The lax laws around personal information facilitated the acts of this man and made it possible for him to stalk and ultimately kill Rebecca Schaeffer. She was taken from the world too soon, as so many people are, and her family and friends continue to mourn her death.

Still, she did not die in vain. As is the case with many people of celebrity status who die, their deaths bring about change. The factors involved in such high profile deaths are examined and laws are put in place to ensure that another does not die for the same reasons.

Rebecca Schaeffer will always be remembered through film and through the legislative changes her death brought forth. It may be little comfort to her family, but it may have saved the lives of countless individuals in the time since.

LAILA KHAN

SARAH THOMERSON

When someone disappears, there is a whole mess of factors to consider. Sometimes, it's a simple as someone stepping out of their old lives and into a new one. Other times, the disappearance smacks of something much more sinister. In history, whole families have vanished out of thin air. Mothers and children have gotten into a car, and driven away, never to be seen again. What makes these cases so startling is the lack of understanding, the denial of closure. Where do these people go? What happens to them? Are they safe?

These are questions that no many people can answer. Sometimes, clues left behind tell a story of what had transpired. Other times, everyone left behind are simply that: left behind. The story of Laila Khan had been a story of disappearance, at first. That is until something much more unsettling was revealed.

For Laila, there's not much information available about her childhood, and how she grew up. What is known, is that she was born Reshma Patel. Her family life is unknown, though Laila did have an older sister by the name of Hashina, and two twin siblings called Zara and Imran. She was a beautiful young woman, there was no denying that. Laila had light skin and dark hair, with big, dark eyes. Her expressions in photographs were often accompanied by a delicate smile. There is such an unsettling lack of information about Laila Khan to be found online. Almost everything has to do with Laila Khan and what happened to her. Even her IMDB page is nothing more than a single sentence.

Perhaps it was Laila's wish to not be known in the spotlight. Perhaps, even, she wasn't all that popular in the film industry. Maybe her family didn't wish to have information about her floating around. Whatever the reason, there isn't much to find about Laila Khan. We can only imagine what her childhood would have been like, with a mother who had two previous husbands and a boyfriend. We can never know how Laila Khan felt about her birth father or her stepfather. There's no information on how she got along with her siblings, or what inspired and drove her to become an actress. All the information that we have of Laila Khan is her sparse Wikipedia entry and the details that followed her disappearance.

Still, Laila Khan was a daughter, a sister, and a friend. She was someone who deserved to have her story told as much as anyone else. While the pieces may be hard to put together, there's still a story somewhere in all of the mess the followed.

Laila Khan was an actress. She was most well known for her work in Bollywood, though with only one film under her belt, Laila couldn't quite be called "famous". Bollywood is Hindi cinema, based mostly out of Mumbai in Maharashtra, India. Because Mumbai was formerly known as Bombay, the term 'Bollywood' comes from the words 'Bombay' and 'Hollywood'.

Bollywood, and Indian Cinema altogether, is incredibly popular. They churn out just under 2,000 feature films, annually. Bollywood, as of 2017, had produced 364 Hindi films - the largest and most popular in the Indian Cinema. Mostly, Bollywood films consist of love triangles, comedic situations, and musical numbers. Laila Khan was just one of many actresses that made Bollywood their home.

What made Laila Khan unique was her alleged marriage to Munir Khan. Munir Khan was, allegedly, a member of the Harkat-ul-Jihad al-Islami. Also abbreviated to HuJI, it meant "Islamic Jihad Movement". It was banned in Bangladesh, and it was an Islamic fundamentalist organization. HuJI had been active since the early 90s and had been banned in Bangladesh since 2005. Its banishment was due to its designation by Bangladesh, as well as several other countries, as a terrorist organization.

HuJI did, indeed, admit to a fundamentalist Islam that had also been taken up by the Taliban. In Bangladesh, HuJI made several assassination attempts on humanists, prime ministers, and other people of importance throughout the 90s and early 2000s. It was no wonder that Laila's alleged marriage to Munir Khan stirred up some talk. Like most of the women in her life, however, Laila's first marriage didn't last. It seemed she was almost more well known for that than she was for her role in Wafa: A Deadly Love Story that she participated in, in 2008. Despite most people knowing Laila from her role in that film, it was considered a failure at the box office. There were very few positive reviews for both the film and Laila Khan's part in it. How poorly the movie did is one of the reasons that Laila Khan is so well known for her role in it.

Laila Khan would become famous for more than just her marriage, and her role in a mediocre Bollywood movie. In February of 2011, Laila drove with her mother, Shelia, her sister Hashmina, her twin siblings, and her cousin, Reshma, out of Mumbai. They were headed to their vacation home, located in Igatpuri. Their vacation home was about 120 km or so north of Mumbai. The family stayed there for a while, at least a week or so. The last known correspondence with them was Shelina, calling her sister and Laila's aunt, Albana Patel. The two sisters spoke about the goings on in the family, and how Laila was currently in Chandigarh, which her third husband, Pervez Iqbal Tak.

This was the last that the family was ever heard from. After that, the entire family - those who had gone the vacation home - completely disappeared.

When a person goes missing, the police and investigators usually look to the people closest to them. In other words, family members become prime suspects. However, when a whole family goes missing, it becomes much more complicated than that. After the family had gone missing, it was actually a television news reported by the name of Nishat Shamsi, that had originally sraised the red flags about Laila Khan's disappearance. It was Shamsi who had first gone to the police in Oshiwara, where Laila lived, to file a missing person's report. Originally, the police refused to entertain the idea. After that, Shamsi decided to investigate Laila's disappearance himself.

Shamsi then took himself to Laila's home. He poked around and began speaking with her neighbors. Her neighbors said that no, they hadn't seen Laila in a while. This seemed suspicious to Shamsi, who decided to look deeper into what was going on. It wasn't until August of 2011, several long months after anyone last heard from Laila Khan or her family, that Shamsi went to speak to Rakesh Sawant. Rakesh Sawant, a Bollywood film director, had been shooting Laila on his second film, Jinnat. They had been working together just before she had left for vacation with her family. Shamsi asked Sawant if he has any idea where Laila Khan was, and he didn't. Together, both Sawant and Shamsi attempt to get in contact with her. But there was no luck - Laila Khan couldn't be contacted, and the two men still had no idea where in the world she, or her family, could be. Shamsi and Sawant went together to the police, but there was still no luck. They wouldn't hear a missing person complaint from them. Finally, Shamsi ran a story about the whole ordeal, and Laila Khan's father came forward.

Laila Khan's father, Nadir Shah Patel, went to the Mumbai police. He wrote a letter of complaint in December of 2011 - almost an entire year after Laila Khan and her family had initially gone missing. How had an entire family been missing since February of 2011, and a missing person complaint not been filed until December of that same year? How had Laila's father and other family members not been concerned? There would be no answers to this, unfortunately. Still, the complaint has been filed and the police were finally getting involved, thanks to Nishat Shamsi. Another story was run by Shamsi in March of 2012, and finally, police got registered the missing person complaint. Over a year later after Laila Khan had gone missing.

Unfortunately, police work was sloppy, to say the least. Both the Oshiwara and Igatpuri police had a lot of shoddy police work under their belts when it came to handling the Laila Khan case. It was only after repeated complaints from Laila's father that the police finally lodged the missing person's investigation. The primary investigation done of the house in Igatpuri found blood stains all over, along with purses and make-up boxes that had never been actually taken by the police. The police also declined to interview people who had last seen Laila and her family, as well as her neighbors and people who knew her.

During their investigation, the main suspects to Laila and her family's disappearance were Parvez Iqbal Tak and Asif Sheikh. Tak was Laila's step-faster, and Sheikh was Shelina's second husband. But the investigation led nowhere. For a year, Laila Khan and her family simply remained a mystery, having disappeared from their vacation home. The rest of their families could do nothing but wonder and worry. It wasn't until July 3rd of 2012 that the case began to move forward. In July, the case was transferred to the Mumbai Police Crime Branch. This came after an arrest was finally made by the Jammu and Kashmir Police.

Parvez Iqbal Tak was arrested and questioned. Finally, he gave up the information that the police needed to start to put together what had happened that day in February.

First, Tak talked about having only killed Laila. His original confession to police insisted that Laila wanted to sell her jewelry before leaving on a trip to Dubai. He admitted to collecting Laila, killing her, and then taking her body back to Igatpuri. This information prompted police to believe that Laila could still be alive somewhere. Police sources insisted that Laila would have worked alongside Tak to be able to gain access to the family property. Of course, nothing more could be said about that until Laila, dead or alive, was found. Finally, Tak gave the police the whole story of what happened to Laila and her family, and where they had really disappeared to.

According to Tak, the family had a barbecue on February 8th, 2011. The evening was just like any other. Laila and her family danced to music, enjoying the evening with family and food. The evening proceeded this way until it was time for bed. The family all went to their separate rooms, which were located on the first floor of the vacation home. It was around one in the morning when they all went to sleep.

However, the night didn't end there. Sometime later, Shelina and Parvez Tak began to argue. The argument was heated and moved through the house. The two went down to the ground floor of the house and it was there, Tak admitted, that he struck Shelina over the head with, what described, as a "blunt object". The commotion drew out the rest of the family, as well as a man by the name of Shakir Hussain, who was staying there as the watchman. Shelina's injuries from the blow to the head were severe.

After seeing what had happened, the rest of the family tried to intervene. According to Tak, he called out to Shakir Hussain. After that, the two of them dispatched the entire family. Together, they killed Laila, her mother, her sister, her twin siblings, and her cousin. But why? What could have driven Tak to murder his wife, his step-children? Could an argument really lead to such a terrible fate?

From the ending of the barbeque and the family going to be, it only took ninety minutes for Laila Khan and her family to meet a fate they could never have anticipated.

Parvez Tak had been living with Shehlina since 2009. As the police interrogated him, more information about the family and all their secrets began to come out. The vacation had been planned out, with Shehlina, Tak and Reshma making their way to the vacation home in Igatpuri before the rest of the family. They stayed there until February 7th, and when they returned, Laila and her twin siblings were ready to go as well. They all went together to Igatpuri. Despite having lived with Shehlina for some time, Tak was still insecure about her close relationship with her second husband. He was also upset about the family's plans to move from Mumbai to Dubai. The plans came about after Laila announced that she planned to marry her current boyfriend, Wafi Khan. At the time, Tak didn't have a passport. He wouldn't be able to come with them, and to him, it felt like a betrayal. Tak felt as if he were being abandoned.

It was Asif Sheikh, Shehlina's second husband, that Shehlina and Tak got into an argument over that night at the vacation house. Recently, Shehlina had turned over power of attorney of her assets to her second husband. This wasn't the first argument about Shiekh that Tak and Shehlina had gotten into. It was just the latest in a long line of arguments, where Tak resented Shehlina's good relationship with her ex, and her praise of him as a person. In fact, even though Tak and Shehlina had been together for two years prior to that fateful evening, Shehlina still hadn't divorced Shiekh.

This was what lead to Tak striking his lover over the head with a "blunt object". It was later discovered that the object that had been used to kill Shehlina was an iron rod. The force of the blow caused her skull to fracture. According to Tak's confession, Shehlina died almost instantly. When the rest of the family came to see what had happened, Tak murdered them for witnessing what they had done, with the help of Shakir Hussain. After detailing all of his crimes to the police, Tak lead them to the vacation house - a farmhouse in Igatpuri.

Himanshu Roy, the Joint Commissioner of Police was lead, along with the Mumbai police, to where Tak had disposed over the bodies that night. Due to the length of time between the murders and Parvez Tak actually confessing to the crimes, there was nothing left of the family but bones. The skeletons of Laila Khan and her family were found piled in a pit at the farmhouse. At the very body, three of the skeletons were found. On top of them, Shahabad stones - or, square, flat flooring stones - had been piled to hide the bodies.

Placed on top of the stones were mattresses soaked with blood, along with clothes and pillows. There, three more skeletons were placed, then covered with one more layer of Shabhabad stones, as well as dirt and mud. The pit that the family had been hidden in was at least six feet deep in the ground, and 12 feet by 8 feet wide and long. Tak stated that he had put the stones in the pit in order to make sure no wild animals came to dig up the bodies.

The skeletons were found with very little clothing. However, police were able to determine that the family was buried with pieces of jewelry still intact, as pieces of necklaces and bracelets were found in the hole. Of the bodies, there was one male and five females, which matches the family members who had gone missing the year previously. Police were able to determine that only Irman, the male twin, had been struck with a heavy object. Otherwise, the women had been disposed of with knives and iron rods.

Of course, DNA tests had to be run on both the weapons found at the farmhouse, as well as the skeletons in the pit. Though police believed that they had found Laila Khan and her family, they still needed to be sure. DNA evidence showed that Reshma, Imran, and Zara were put in the bottom of the put before being covered by the stones and blood-stained sheets and mattresses. The other bodies were placed on top of them, including Laila Khan. Still on her body's finger was a diamond ring that had been gifted to Laila by her then boyfriend.

Here is where the breadcrumbs of Laila Khan's story lead. She was a beloved sister and daughter, and an actress that had not yet had her time to shine. Like a light, she had been extinguished by a man who was jealous and greedy. After having witnessed her mother's death, Laila, along with her family members, were executed by a man that they were supposed to trust not to harm them.

Unfortunately, Laila Khan's story is not so unique, except perhaps because she was an actress. There are many women in India just like Laila Khan - disappeared without a trace, with no media outrage to spark the police into finding them. According to statistics, just over a third of women in India report some form of domestic violence. Of course, many of these women lead relatively normal lives - they're mothers and wives, not daughters of multimillionaires. Parvez Tak struck out against Laila Khan's mother because he was jealous of her relationship with another man in her life, and felt he was losing control over her, and the family. They were planning on moving without him, and so he did the only thing he could think of to stop it from happening.

Thankfully, in the years following Laila Khan's death, there has been a push in India to protect women from domestic violence. The police muddled through the disappearance of Laila and her family, but hopefully, they will have learned from those mistakes. While Laila's case may not have been typical, the world is working on changing the circumstances that made Tak's execution of the family possible. As for Laila Khan, the most that can be done for her now is to share her story.

THE MURDER OF ADRIENNE SHELLY

22

JOSEPH REMAR

Adrienne Shelly was born Adrienne Levine, on June 24th 1966. She was born in Queens, and remained a native of there throughout her childhood. Her parents were Sheldon M. Levine and Elaine Langbaum, and she was raised with her two brothers Jeff and Mark. Her childhood was apparently happy and stable.

Her entrance into the world of the performing arts came at the age of just 10. Her career began at the Stagedoor Manor Performing Arts Training Center, where she learned her craft, before making her professional debut in a rendition of the musical Annie while she was still a high school student. Adrienne took her professional surname (Shelly) from her father's given name, Sheldon. Her father had died when Shelly was aged 12.

After graduation, she left New York for Boston University, where she majored in film production. She didn't enjoy her time there, however, and she dropped out after her junior year and moved back to Manhattan to start her career. Her first forays were into indie movies, and she became reasonably well-known for her femme-fatale characters, although by all accounts, she was more of a "clown" in real life.

Shelly was not just successful in her own right, as her husband was successful too. She married Andy Ostroy, who is still chairman and CEO of Belardi/Ostroy, a marketing firm. The pair met shortly after September 11th, which was a strange time to live in New York. They had been set up on a date by matchmaking friends. "I didn't really know what to make of her at first," Ostroy later recalled. "She was like no one I'd ever met. But I knew right away that she was special. There are very few people in this world who are really unique, and she touched you in a way that meant you could never forget her. It's hard to explain. She had a big smile and a genius IQ."

The couple had a daughter together in 2003, who was named Sophie, and had only turned two by the time that Shelly died. Shelly was killed in a senseless robbery at the apartment she used as her office, late in 2006.

Successful career

Shelly's big break came in 1989, when she was 23 years of age. She was cast in her first leading role in Hal Hartley's independent film, The Unbelievable Truth. Just a year later, she teamed up with Hartley again, this time for the lead role in Trust. Both films were financial successes, and Trust was even nominated for the Grand Jury Prize at the Sundance Film Festival, where Hartley was a joint winner of a scriptwriting award. Meanwhile, Shelly broke through on TV as well as at the box office. She landed roles in several hit TV shows like Law & Order, Oz and Homicide: Life on the Street.

Not content with how well she was doing on screen, Shelly took to the stage, taking on roles in at least two dozen off-Broadway plays. She set up a theater company called Missing Children in 1996. She performed most often at the Manhattan Guesthouse Theater, and played there throughout her long career.

But rather than push on with her well-received start in the film industry, Shelly decided to move instead into roles behind the camera. One of her first successes was I'll Take You There, a 1999 comedy starring Ally Sheedy. For her direction of the movie, Shelly received a U.S. Comedy Arts Festival Film Discovery Jury Award in 2000. She also won Best Director for the same movie at the Tróia International Film Festival.

Her final contribution to film was the movie Waitress. "The central theme of the film is what Adrienne felt in her own life," Shelly's husband told People Magazine. "This story is about a woman who is afraid. It's about a woman who has real challenges and fears in life.

Adrienne was worried that having a child, even though she was still having the child relatively late in life, would jeopardise her career. "There's a moment where Keri Russell finds out that she's pregnant and she's not happy. The doctor even says, 'Uncongratulations.' That was pretty much what Adrienne had feared – that would she lose her identity as a person and her ability to work."

But in a familiar story to parents who at one time had trepidations about having children for the first time, Shelly's outlook completely changed after her daughter's birth. "Once she saw Sophie, it was incredible. The love she had for that child was just monumental. Her fears vanished. She just adored that little girl so much."

And Shelly's fears about being unable to juggle children and career were completely unfounded. "When she started editing the film, she would be in her old apartment where she went to write," he says. "Sophie would be crawling around the floor while she was editing and working on the script. She was joyful about being able to achieve her dreams and still be a mother who was still madly in love with her child. She finally had it all."

The movie was released in 2007, which starred Nathan Fillion and Keri Russell (and Shelly's daughter Sophie, who appeared in a cameo role towards the end of the film). It premiered that year at the Sundance Film Festival. She wrote and directed the movie, and coordinated both set and costume design as well. But unfortunately, she didn't live to see the success of her final creation.

Death ruled suicide

In what was a shock to her family and to the film-going public, Shelly was found dead on the evening of November 1st, 2006. She was discovered in the bathroom of the apartment she used as an office in Manhattan's West Village, hanging from a shower rail with a bedsheet around her neck.

Unfortunately, she was found by her husband, Andy Ostroy. He had suspected that something was amiss; after he had dropped her off early that morning, she hadn't contacted him for the entire day. Ostroy dropped by that evening to see if anything was the matter, and brought the doorman with him in case of intruders.

There were no signs of forced entry, and the door was unlocked, so they went inside. Instead of finding intruders (or indeed anything that might suggest foul play) they found Shelly alone in her apartment, already dead.

Investigations began immediately. The NYPD immediately found that some money had been stolen, or at least home missing, from Shelly's wallet. But they didn't find any other clues that might have suggested anything other than suicide. An autopsy, unsurprisingly, found that the cause of death had been strangulation.

Footprints found

This version of events wasn't enough for Ostroy. He knew for a fact that Shelly had been happy in both her work and her personal life, and that she was the last person who would leave a two year old without a mother. "There's no way on this planet that she would have left that child," he said. "Nobody is ever going to tell me that woman walked away from Sophie." Something didn't add up, and Ostroy pushed the NYPD to resume their analysis of the crime scene.

Taking him at his word, the NYPD did a second sweep of the bathroom for any extra clues. Their efforts revealed something they hadn't seen before: a muddy shoe print, outlined in gypsum powder, on the toilet seat. The pattern didn't match any of Shelly's shoes, nor of Ostroy's; this, therefore, was their first lead. Expanding their search, the NYPD investigators noticed that the print matched another set found elsewhere in the building, where construction work had been taking place on the day of Shelly's death.

They had examined the shoes of every single person who was known to have entered the apartment that day, including even emergency workers and police officers, but had found no matches. They expanded their search to include the rest of the building, and found that the construction work had been taking place; they then noticed that a set of footprints outlined on one of the work sites was a perfect match for the one in Shelly's bathroom.

Worker charged

It took the NYPD five days until they thought they had their man. On November 6th, 2006, Diego Pillco was arrested and charged with the murder of Adrienne Shelly. Pillco was an illegal immigrant, originally from Ecuador, who had been working on the construction site that day. Pillco lived on Prospect Avenue in Greenwood Heights, Brooklyn, at the time that he was arrested. He had only arrived in the city, having come straight from Ecuador, that July. Investigators had tracked him down, and identified him as the wanted man based on the footprints they had found.

He was taken that day from his apartment block, to a waiting police car. The press had already picked up that this may have been the man suspected of Shelly's murder- so Pillco left the building escorted by police officers, wearing a Yankees cap low over his face to avoid photographers.

Investigators reported that he had confessed to the murder. "He admits to hitting her, believes he had killed her and wanted to fake her suicide," one of the investigators told the press the day after Pillco's arrest. He asked not to be named since investigations were, at that point, still continuing. "It appeared to be a suicide — he staged it as a suicide," the investigator said. But his team had "never just accepted it for what it was staged to be."

Speaking after Pillco had been charged, Shelly's agent Rachel Sheedy said: "We have felt adamantly that what happened was not the result of suicide. It is a great relief knowing that the police have taken us seriously." Neighbors of Pillco's also spoke to the press, shortly after he was first charged. They expressed their shock at the difference between the criminal that they read about in the newspapers, and the neighbor they had lived next to all that time.

"He sent money home to his mother and father," said Frank Lingo, who lived nearby. "He minded his business. He never bothered me or anyone else near here. He seemed like a good kid. I've never seen him hang out." Chris Pannhorse, another of Pillco's neighbors, told the press that "He was always respectful to me and my wife. He's a good kid. Because that is what he is to me, just a kid."

What had happened that day?

According to Pillco's initial version of events, Shelly had asked him to 'keep the noise down' since she had been working in her office that day. Taking offence to her, Pillco threw a hammer at her out of anger. Pillco had been working on an apartment on the third floor, directly below the apartment that Shelly used as her office.

He confessed that because of his poor grasp of English, he had been unable to fully understand what she was saying; but he had picked up on the fact that she had threatened to call the police. After she had run back to her apartment, Pillco followed her. He said that he had been afraid she would make a complaint to his superior, or to call 911, which would result in his sacking and the revelation of his status as an illegal immigrant.

Out of fear, therefore, Pillco said that he had killed Shelly that day. In the ensuing struggle once they reached her office, Shelly hit him, but Pillco hit back harder, and Shelly fell awkwardly and died. He was unsure as to whether the blow had killed her, but nevertheless, he confessed to staging the scene to make it appear like a simple suicide.

Friends and family of Shelly were grateful to Ostroy, as they felt that none of the real story would have come out had it not been for his efforts in convincing investigators to look harder. "He was her hero," a friend of Shelly, Sasha Eden, told the press, "even in her death. Andy did everything in his power, and made the whole murder come out."

Conflicting stories

However, by the time of his trial, Pillco's story had changed entirely. In truth, Pillco's first story did seem to be inconsistent in places: for instance, while he claimed that Shelly had come screaming into the building site that he was working on, Shelly's shoes had been completely clean when they were assessed by investigators.

He initially plead not guilty, but eventually gave damning testimony against himself during proceedings after agreeing to a plea bargain. He later said that he had simply seen her while he was on his break, and taken the elevator to her apartment with the intent of either assaulting her or stealing her purse: he was never completely clear.

Finding that she wasn't there, Pillco decided to take advantage of the situation. He rifled through Shelly's purse, stealing some money; but he was discovered in the act. Shelly confronted him, and perhaps scratched him; similarly to events in his first confession, she then picked up the phone to try to call 911. Pillco grabbed the phone to stop her.

But Shelly wasn't afraid to call for help, and Pillco hit her hard, knocking her to the ground.

"So out of desperation, I got scared and I covered her mouth," Pillco told the packed courtroom during his trial. It was this that had rendered Shelly unconscious. "When I noticed she fell to the floor, I was very scared. When she fell to the floor, I saw a sheet, and I decided to choke her — and that's what happened." The judge cut across him to ask: "And then you tied the sheet around her neck and you strung her up?"

"Si," Pillco replied. "Yes, and I made it look like it was suicide."

After strangling her until she was unconscious, he set up the fake suicide scene. It was the weight of her body pulling the bed sheet tight around her neck that eventually killed her. This was confirmed at trial by the medical examiner, who stated that Shelly had been alive at the time she was left hanging in the bathroom; it had therefore been the cover-up that had killed her, not the initial fight.

Because he had not delivered the final killing blow, Pillco was offered a plea of first degree manslaughter. Prosecutors feared that they may have been unsuccessful if they tried to find him guilty of murder, because of the chance that he would switch to his original story again.

It almost seemed too soon after proceedings had begun, just four months earlier, for the trial to be at an end in February. He had been offered a plea by the Manhattan district attorney, who recognised the shakiness of Pillco's story. In return for pleading guilty to a charge of first-degree manslaughter, he would receive a set sentence of 25 years. Considering that he could have potentially been found guilty of murder in a trial by jury, Pillco's lawyers insisted that he grab the offer with both hands.

Pillco, for his part, did show remorse at the end of the hearings. "If there were a death penalty, I would take it," he told the courtroom though an interpreter.. "All I want to say is I know they're not going to forgive me. This is what I deserve." But Shelly's family, who were in the courtroom looking down at Pillco, couldn't have appeared any less forgiving. Elaine was sobbing, wiping her eyes, and hissing "No... No!"-

she could not forgive the man who had murdered her daughter. Neither could any other member of her family, nor could Andy Ostroy- it was simply too soon.

In response to Pillco's please for forgiveness, even the judge retorted: "I don't think you'll get that, sir."

It seemed so senseless, and so strange that a man who could show such remorse could have killed Shelly the way that he had. But according to the evidence, testimony and his own confessions, he had committed the crime. He was given a sentence of 25 years, with no chance of parole, and a practical guarantee that he would be deported back to Ecuador upon his release.

Ostroy speaks out against his wife's killer

During the hearing at which Pillco's sentence was handed down, Andy Ostroy was given a chance to speak his mind- and he took his chance to express the anger, hurt and loss he had felt after his wife's senseless murder. "No sentence will be enough for you. You deserve the same fate you handed Adrienne. I want you to suffer like she suffered."

"You are nothing more than a cold-blooded killer, a murderous beast who in an intent to rob, rape and then silence your innocent victim ... took the life of a beautiful, loving woman who, unlike you, had so much to give to society," he said, glaring down at Pillco, who couldn't meet his gaze.

"You stalked and brutally attacked my wife, silenced her screams with your hand until you rendered her unconscious and then, in a brutal and gruesome act of cowardice, took a bedsheet and strangled her to death," Ostroy said, still staring as if unable to wrench his eyes away from his wife's killer. "You tied her up and hung her the way you strung up pigs back in Ecuador."

Shelly's mother, Elaine Langbaum, was also given a chance to speak. She used her time to talk about how Shelly and her daughter, after such a perfect start in life, had been robbed of their chance to grow older together. "The baby she wanted for so long will never know her mother," she said. "She will never hold her mother's hand, kiss her mother's face or feel her mother's hug."

Ostroy sues the construction company

After taking time to grieve, and recover as much as he could, Ostroy decided that he hadn't finished trying to make sense of Shelly's death. He has described himself as "a born and bred New Yorker- push me and I'll push back harder," and he felt a need to find justice. He decided to sue the construction company that had hired Pillco, and demanded a settlement for a charge of negligence.

However, the Appellate Division of the Manhattan court system decided to uphold the earlier decision ruling against Ostroy's suit. They unanimously judged that the construction company were innocent of the charge, since murder was not a part of Pillco's job description, and therefore his actions could not be judged the liability of the company. The judges agreed that there was no way that the construction company could have identified Pillco's propensity for violence upon hiring him, and that he had been furthering his own interests in killing Shelly, not those of the company.

While in hindsight, a successful suit always seemed unlikely, Ostroy's actions make sense in the context of grief and loss. He had lashed out in an attempt to find somebody else to blame. Pillco was in prison, having been found guilty, and even having shown remorse; but his crime had been so mindless, shocking and unpredictable that it must have been difficult for the family to make sense of his actions.

Waitress

Shelly's final movie, Waitress, was also her final and best success. It premiered at the Sundance Film Festival in 2007, to a rapturous reception. "Seeing Waitress at Sundance was a really emotional experience,' said Nancy Utley, a CEO at Fox Searchlight, which was one of the distributers that had bid for rights to the film. "The typical format for the festival is that the director is introduced to say a few words before the film begins. It was painful from the beginning to see that there was no director to introduce the film, since Adrienne had passed away. So the producer and Adrienne's husband Andy talked about how it had been Adrienne's dream to have a film at Sundance. It was very poignant."

According to Utley, the film was exceptionally well-received. "The movie played like gangbusters. The audience was laughing and crying, and sometimes both at the same time. There was a standing ovation at the end." There was also a political/societal point that could be made of the film: Shelly had written, edited and directed Waitress while pregnant and just after having given birth. This was in addition to all the challenges that she, as a woman, had to overcome. "No one questions Woody Allen or Christopher Guest," Sasha Eden said after the movie's success. "But when you're a woman it's much more challenging. Here was this gorgeous writer-director-actor who had to constantly prove that she could do it."

The movie's producer, Michael Roiff, completely agreed. "One of the things she was most excited about was the fact that she had done this as a woman and as a mother. She was an amazing mum, and I remember one day when we had watched a cut of the film, she turned around and said: "Look, you can do it. Society wants to tell you that you have to choose, but you don't have to choose.""

During the movie's success, Broadway producers Barry and Fran Weissler saw a screening and decided to turn it into a musical number. The show was a hit. "When I found out it was heading to Broadway, I was thrilled," Ostroy said afterwards "When I look at Adrienne's life, career and legacy, she had this film that did really well, is now on Broadway and she has impacted the lives of so many female filmmakers. I have seen that out of tragedy, something really good can come, otherwise it's all in vain. Her murder didn't stop her from going on, even if in name only."

Ostroy and Sophie have since seen the show, and described it as "a wonderful addition to Adrienne's legacy. It's one of the many things she has to remember about her mother as she is growing up."

Shelly's foundation

Shelly's husband was also determined that some good should come from his wife's early death. "For a few weeks after she died, I had a lot of people who were asking where they could donate money in her honor," he says. "It was too soon. I didn't know. Those first few weeks were harrowing and I wanted to think about it. When my head was able to get clearer, I thought, 'What would Adrienne want? Who would Adrienne want to help?' Other struggling women filmmakers."

"'I think Adrienne would be very proud that in her name other women are being helped in ways that she wished she could have been. Given what happened to her, there's so much positive that can come out of it - that's the reason behind the foundation: to try to take something horrible and make something positive."

He set up a foundation in her name, the aim of which was to provide women in the showbusiness industry with a leg-up that could help their careers. The board are such Hollywood stars as Cheryl Hines, Paul Rudd and Michelle Williams, and so far the foundation has teamed up with production studios and organisations like the American Film Institute, the Sundance Film Festival, Women in Film, the Tribeca Film Institute and Rooftop Films.

They have given out at least 60 production grants since the foundation's inception, one of the most successful being a grant for filmmaker Cynthia Wade in 2007. The grant helped her to release the documentary film Freeheld, which was given an Academy Award. Speaking about his organisation's helping hand for Cynthia Wade, Ostroy claimed: "She said she couldn't have made that film without our support. To help a filmmaker win an Academy Award with help from our foundation made us realize the impact that we could have – and so soon."

He continued, "Starting the foundation was the right thing to do for Adrienne and the right thing to do, period. I think Adrienne would have loved that we are helping filmmakers like her in her honor and in her name."

THE MURDER OF DOMINIQUE DUNNE

ERICA THOMAS

Destined for stardom

In November 1959, film producer Dominick Dunne and actress Ellen (Lenny) Dunne welcomed a new baby to their growing family. Dominique Dunne was the couple's youngest of three children, and their only daughter. Dunne and her older brothers grew up surrounded by the arts – in addition to the influence of their parents, who were active in the California film industry, the children were frequently surrounded by celebrities of the 50s and 60s – close family friends who were often guests at the family home.

Dunne and her siblings grew up in a large house in Beverly Hills, but moved around fairly frequently as Dunne attended schools across the country – in Los Angeles, Connecticut, and Colorado. However, Dunne's childhood wasn't entirely carefree – when she was just eleven years old, Dunne's parents divorced. A few years later, in 1975, her mother was diagnosed with multiple sclerosis.

Still, Dunne pursued her education. After her graduation in 1977, Dunne studied art and Italian in Florence, at the Michelangelo School and at the British Institute. When she returned to California, she worked briefly as a receptionist and translator for Los Angeles' Italian Trade Commission before venturing back to Ft. Collins to study acting at the Colorado State University.

Her studies in Colorado were short-lived, however, and Dunne left after only one year to start auditioning back in California. Just a few weeks later, she was offered her very first film role. Dunne's acting career took off quite quickly – in her first three years, Dunne appeared as a guest on many well-known television shows, including *Family*, *CHiPs*, and *Fame*. And after taking on roles in four made-for-TV movies, Dunne made her cinematic debut as Dana Freeling in the movie "Poltergeist."

"One day, she decided to become an actress and the next week she was on a back lot making a movie, and that from then on she never stopped," said Dunne's father Dominick in a piece he wrote for Vanity Fair in March 1984. "She loved being an actress and was passionate about her career."

"At ease in a sophisticated world."

To her friends and family, Dunne was known as a friendly, kind person. Despite having grown up with wealth and fame, Dunne's father described her as "totally at ease in a sophisticated world without being sophisticated herself." Indeed, Dunne dressed in casual clothes, preferring jeans and t-shirts to the upscale fashions her peers sported – and drove a blue Volkswagen Bug convertible.

Dunne loved cooking, traveling, baseball, and languages – particularly Italian, which she continued to speak quite fluently. She also loved animals, and had a soft spot for unwanted strays. Dunne adopted a cat with a lobotomy, a large dog with stunted legs, a snake, and a rabbit, among many other cats and dogs.

Even before her role in "Poltergeist," Dunne was a firm believer in supernatural phenomena, and friends say she was strictly superstitious.

Instant attraction

Dunne met John Thomas Sweeney in 1981, when she was twenty-two and he was twenty-five. Sweeney worked as a chef at Los Angeles' trendy "Ma Maison" restaurant, and Dunne was immediately drawn to him. After their initial introduction at a party that autumn, the pair quickly fell into a romantic relationship – and moved in together only a few weeks later, into a rental house in West-Hollywood.

However, their passion soon resulted in the first of many quarrels between the couple. Dunne was, by that point, well-known in Hollywood – a popular girl with many friends. Sweeney, on the other hand, had grown up poor in Pennsylvania, the product of a troubled family life. Despite Dunne's attempts to include him in her world, Sweeney felt like an outsider and was ashamed of his uncultured family history.

While Dunne had grown up with a loving family that respected and addressed emotional issues, Sweeney was raised in a coal town with an alcoholic father who, his mother claimed, often dealt with his frustrations by beating her – often in front of their children. By the time he was fourteen years old, his parents had divorced, and his father had developed epilepsy.

"Bitterly ashamed of his family and filled with a sense of worthlessness because he was a member of it, (Sweeney) longed to escape into a larger and more exciting life," read an article published in *People* magazine in 1983.

Sweeney's desire for a better life led him to pursue a culinary arts diploma from a local community college. At the age of twenty, he crossed the country to California, where he landed a job working at a restaurant called "Picolo's." Only one year later, he started as a chef's apprentice at "Ma Maison."

He was a talented, ambitious chef – and was willing to put in the work to achieve his career goals. After two years of double shifts, Sweeney was given a leave of absence to spend a year working on the French Riviera before returning to "Ma Maison" – where he worked as chef Wolfgang Puck's chief assistant.

His position at the glamorous restaurant gave him an opportunity to get a first-hand look at the elegant world he so desperately wanted to be a part of. And, after meeting Dunne, he finally felt like he would be able to access it. However, along with his excitement at being with a talented Hollywood actress, there was fear and insecurity – and the lasting sense of worthlessness he felt as a result of his troubled family life.

His jealousy started to take hold of the relationship. His interactions with Dunne grew more patronizing and dominating, and he began showing up on sets where Dunne was working to intimidate her male colleagues. Eventually, even that wasn't enough – Sweeney started to come to Dunne's rehearsals and even her acting classes.

It seemed Dunne couldn't do anything on her own without having to first discuss it with her boyfriend, which usually resulted in an argument that Dunne would never win. The more Dunne resisted Sweeney's possessiveness and jealousy, the more frightened he would be that she would ultimately reject him. Often, this fear would become anger.

"Alex said he was scary."

Dunne had introduced Sweeney to her family during the summer of 1982, flying the two of them out to New York where most of her family lived. According Dominick's article in Vanity Fair, Dunne's brother Alex was the only one who had "voiced his dislike" of her new boyfriend.

"Although I could see that Sweeney was excessively devoted to her, there was something off-putting about him," Dominick said.

The first night, Alex told his father about an incident that had happened after Dominick had left the restaurant. Dunne had been recognized by a man in the bar, who called out her iconic line from the film "Poltergeist." According to Alex, "there was no flirtation," just an excited, if slightly tipsy, fan.

"When Sweeney returned to the table and saw the man talking to (Dunne), he became enraged. He picked up the man and shook him," stated Dominick. "Alex said that Sweeney's reaction was out of all proportion to the incident going on. Alex said he was scary."

The next day, Dominick was to meet Dunne and Sweeney for lunch. Although he said he arrived at the restaurant late, the couple still wasn't there – and Dominick was already on his second bottle of Perrier by the time his daughter showed up with her boyfriend.

"I was immediately aware that she had been crying, and that there was tension between them," Dominick said. "The lunch was not a success. I found Sweeney ill at ease, nervous, difficult to talk to. It occurred to me that (Dunne) might have difficulty extricating herself from such a person, but I did not pursue the thought."

Getting physical

As the couple began fighting more and more, Sweeney's reactions frequently turned violent. On August 27, 1982, Sweeney reportedly tore out handfuls of Dunne's hair after grabbing it and using it to knock her head repeatedly against the floor. Dunne managed to get away from Sweeney and fled to her mother Lenny's house, with Sweeney following close behind. While Dunne's mother refused him entry and even threatened to call the police, it was only a few days before Dunne forgave her boyfriend and returned to their home.

Despite Dunne's forgiveness, Sweeney attacked her again not even a month later. On September 26, during another argument, Sweeney grabbed Dunne by the neck and pushed her to the floor before he started to choke her. Luckily, a friend heard the loud gagging noises coming from the next room – "it was the worst sound I had ever heard" – and came in to break up the fight.

"He tried to kill me!" Dunne cried out. Sweeney denied her accusation, insisting that Dunne come back to bed. Instead, she went into the bathroom, where she escaped out a window to spend the night with a friend.

The next day, Dunne showed up at the set of *Hill Street Blues*, where she was to guest star as an abuse victim for an episode of the show. According to accounts from cast and crew on the set, the bruises on Dunne's face and neck were "realistic" enough that she hardly needed any make-up for her role.

Dunne spent the following days in hiding, trying to avoid the abusive, angry boyfriend who was searching for her. Eventually, she contacted him to end the relationship – and to demand he leave the home they rented together so she could live there alone. Still, knowing how unpredictably angry and violent Sweeney could be, Dunne changed the locks of the house before moving back in without him.

The final battle

That autumn, Dunne had taken on a new role – playing Robin Maxwell for the three-episode science fiction miniseries *V.* She'd completed filming the scenes for the first episode and was nearly finished with the second episode on October 30, when she invited her co-star David Packer to rehearse scenes together at her home.

The pair were hard at work when Sweeney called Dunne at around 8:30 p.m. – and then showed up at the house only ten minutes later. Dunne answered the door with the chain fastened, but Sweeney demanded she come out and speak with him. Packer asked if he should leave, sensing Dunne's discomfort with the situation, but she said she wanted him to stay while she stepped outside to deal with her ex-boyfriend.

Out on the driveway, an argument broke out. Sweeney was pleading with Dunne to forgive him and take him back, but Dunne refused. She'd reached her limit and was no longer willing to tolerate Sweeney's anger and violence. Like he'd done before, Sweeney suddenly reached out and grabbed her firmly by the neck, dragging her up along the driveway into the next-door neighbour's back yard.

Dunne was no match for Sweeney – the petite actress was a mere 5'1" and 112 pounds. Sweeney, 6'1" and close to 200 pounds, held her down and began to strangle her. She was unable to fight him off, and eventually fell unconscious.

Meanwhile, Packer watched the confrontation with growing fear – he could see Sweeney's obvious rage and jealousy. When he heard screams followed by a thud, he called the police, only to be informed that the location was outside of the department's jurisdiction. After hanging up with the officer, Packer called a friend and left a message on his answering machine explaining that if he was found dead, John Sweeney should be held responsible.

Eventually, Packer went outside to check on Dunne, and found her lying on the driveway with Sweeney crouched next to her. Sweeney asked Dunne to call the police, and this time, they said they would send an officer. When the police arrived and found Dunne still unconscious, they called an ambulance, which arrived only five minutes later.

Brain-dead

On the way to the nearby Cedars Sinai Hospital, Dunne's heart came to a full stop, but doctors were able to restart it once the ambulance arrived. However, examinations showed that Dunne had sustained extensive damage from the anoxaemia during her strangulation – and that although her heart had been restarted, there was no way for doctors to reverse the death of her brain.

"There were tubes in her everywhere, and the life-support system caused her to breathe in and out with a grotesque jerking movement that seemed a parody of life," Dominick recalled. "Her eyes were open, massively enlarged, staring lifelessly up at the ceiling. Her beautiful hair had been shaved off. A large bolt had been screwed into her skull to relieve the pressure on her brain. Her neck was purpled and swollen; vividly visible on it were the marks of the massive hands of the man who had strangled her.

It was nearly impossible to look at her, but also impossible to look away."

The hospital's staff did everything they could for Dunne, and after five days, her parents made the decision to remove her from the life-support systems that were keeping her alive. Dunne died instantly, and her heart and kidneys were donated to the hospital to be used for transplants.

Dunne's tragic death was a shock to the entire Hollywood community, particularly for Dunne's extensive network of family and friends. Hundreds of people attended Dunne's funeral, held on November 6 at the catholic Church of the Good Shepherd in Beverly Hills – the same church where Dunne had been baptized 22 years earlier. Her body was laid to rest near Los Angeles, at the Westwood Memorial Park.

"An act of passion and despair."

"If (Dunne) had been killed in an automobile accident, horrible as that would have been, at least it would have been over and mourning could have begun," Dominick said. "A murder is an ongoing event until the day of the sentencing, and mourning has to be postponed."

Sweeney was charged with Dunne's murder, and the case finally went to trial at the court in Santa Monica in early August, 1983. A *People* magazine article from October 1983 described Sweeney as a "young man in a black suit" seated at a long table, his face "white as an egg" and his large, pale hands "folded meekly" over a Bible.

"It is the fashion among the criminal fraternity to find God, and Sweeney, the killer, was no exception," Dominick remembered. "The Bible was a prop; Sweeney never read it, he just rested his folded hands on it. He also wept regularly. One day, the court had to be recessed because he claimed the other prisoners had been harassing before he entered, and he needed time to cry in private.

"I could not believe that the jurors would buy such a performance."

But Sweeney painted a very different picture in the courtroom than the true colors he'd shown to Dunne's family and friends. According to Sweeney's testimony, Dunne "provoked" the violent struggle that resulted in her death, because she had previously agreed to reconcile and had then refused to take Sweeney back. Sweeney said he "just exploded and lunged toward her" after she told him she'd been lying when she said she would live with him again.

He added that he "had no memory" of the event, only that he found himself next to Dunne's unconscious body, with his hands pressed around her neck. According to Sweeney, he tried to resuscitate her, and when that didn't work, he ran into the house and swallowed two bottles of pills – attempting suicide due to his panic and regret at what he had done.

Sweeney's lawyer Michael Adelson added that Dunne was a "snob," who was constantly telling Sweeney how he was beneath her. Sweeney's account of their relationship presented Dunne as two-faced and heartless, and he said she even told him that she had been leading him on.

Dominick even recalled receiving a phone call from the prosecutor for the case, district attorney Steven Barshop, in July, shortly before the trial was set to begin. Barshop explained that Adelson had requested that Lenny not be allowed in the courtroom – Adelson felt the presence of the victim's mother, confined to a wheelchair, would create "undue sympathy for her that would be prejudicial to Sweeney."

The "accident" was a "tragedy," Adelson argued, "not a real crime – an action of passion and despair."

However, no evidence could be found to back up Sweeney's story, and investigators were reluctant to believe him. There was nothing to support Sweeney's claim that he'd attempted to commit suicide, and even during his initial interrogation, Sweeney seemed to show little remorse for his part in Dunne's death.

In fact, the police officers who arrested him testified that Sweeney had seemed "quite calm and collected," and more concerned about what would happen to him than what had happened to Dunne – only about an hour and a half after he'd been arrested.

"I fucked up, I can't believe I did something that will put me behind bars forever," Sweeney reportedly told police when he was brought down to the station. "Man, I blew it. I killed her. I didn't think I choked her that hard. I just kept on choking her. I just lost my temper and blew it again."

When one of the officers made a comment about how well Dunne had been doing with her acting career, Sweeney retorted, "well, I was doing quite well in *my* career. I'm quite proud of what I've done."

Upon further investigation, it was revealed that Sweeney had obviously strangled Dunne for about five minutes – at least four minutes, according to the medical examiner. According to police, this makes Sweeney's story fairly improbable. Not only would Sweeney have had enough time to realize what he was doing while he was choking his ex-girlfriend, he would have had the opportunity to regain control and let Dunne live.

During the trial, Dominick remembers Barshop holding up a hand to the jury, silencing the room for a four-minute period – "how long it took for Dominique Dunne to die," Barshop said, in his opening statement.

"It was horrifying," Dominick said. "I had never allowed myself to think how long she had struggled in his hands, thrashing for life. A gunshot or a knife stab is over in an instant; strangulation is an eternity."

Barshop also brought forward testimony from one of Sweeney's previous girlfriends – a secretary named Lillian Pierce, who'd also lived with Sweeney. During their relationship, which lasted from 1977 to

1980, he'd abused her on at least ten different occasions – resulting in two separate hospital visits, one for a perforated eardrum and collapsed lung, and a second time with a broken nose.

"Later, we heard that (Pierce) had sat in a car outside the church at (Dunne's) funeral and cried," Dominick said, "feeling too guilty to go inside."

The testimony proved that unlike what Sweeney's lawyer had argued, this was not a unique crime of passion, but rather a pattern of abusive behaviour toward women. Still, Sweeney's lawyer was able to convince the judge that the testimony was prejudicial, and had it excluded from the trial.

"Her account of her relationship with John Sweeney was so shocking that it should have put to rest forever the defense stand that the strangulation death of Dominique Dunne at the hands of John Sweeney was an isolated incident," wrote Dominick. "He was, it became perfectly apparent, a classic abuser of women – and his weapon was his hands."

As he questioned Pierce, without the jury present, Adelson inquired about a specific discussion the witness had had with himself and another lawyer on November 3, 1982 – the day before Dunne was officially removed from life-support and pronounced legally dead.

"Even while (Dunne) lay dying, efforts were being made to free her killer by men who knew very well that this was not his first display of violence," Dominick said. "I felt hatred for Michael Adelson. His object was to win; nothing else mattered."

Testimonies from Dunne's friends and co-workers were also ruled out after Sweeney's lawyer argued that they were nothing but hearsay. These statements explained that Dunne was not remotely interested in a reconciliation with Sweeney – in fact, she'd spent the final five weeks of her life in "permanent fear" of her abusive ex-boyfriend.

Even without this important evidence, the prosecution still sought a second-degree murder conviction, with a minimum sentence of fifteen years.

The jury did get to hear a letter found by Dunne's friends, addressed to Sweeney but obviously never sent to him. The letter detailed Dunne's frustrations at the control Sweeney attempted to hold over her, and her desire to end the relationship.

"You do not love me. You are obsessed with me. The person you think you love is not me at all. It is someone you have made up in your head," Dunne said in her letter. "I'm the person who makes you angry, who you fight with sometimes. I think we only fight when images of me fade away and you are faced with the real me.

"The whole thing has made me realize how scared I am of you, and I don't mean just physically. I'm afraid of the next time you are going to have another mood swing. When we are good, we are great. But when we are bad, we are horrendous. The bad outweighs the good."

An unsatisfying result

The trial wrapped up at the end of September, and the jury found Sweeney guilty of voluntary manslaughter – to the shock of Dunne's family and friends. "The law protected him," the jury said, but several members later admitted that had they known about Sweeney's history of violence and abuse, they would have found him guilty of the second-degree murder charge.

"I guess there is never any real satisfaction that the legal system can give, but this – the outcome – was such a blow, such a slap in the face to our family and to (Dunne's) memory," said Dunne's older brother Griffin. "They literally got away with murder... the bitterness of that will never leave."

Even Superior Court Judge Burton S. Katz, who presided over the trial, felt the system failed to provide justice for Dunne's tragic murder. Barshop stated that this failure has allowed a "time bomb" to return to the streets, where he could potentially abuse again, and blames Katz for the many rulings he made that prohibited the jury from hearing important, relevant evidence.

However, Katz argued that he had no choice but to rule the way he had – but admitted that some of the more controversial rulings during the trial "pained" him. Shortly after Sweeney's trial, Katz moved to the Juvenile Court in Sylmar.

"Nothing is more difficult than rendering a decision based upon a law with which you disagree," Katz said. "Unfortunately, following the letter of the law sometimes doesn't permit one to pursue the ultimate goal of justice."

Sweeney ended up with a sentence of only six and a half years in prison, the maximum sentence imposed for convictions of voluntary manslaughter. Instead of the fifteen years the prosecution had hoped for, Sweeney was released from a medium-security state prison after spending three years, seven months, and twenty-seven days in custody.

"Three and a half years for a life is certainly not justice," Katz said. "If I could have given him 25 (years), I would have given him 25. If I could have given him life, I would have given him life... I agree with everyone that based on his past record of violence... he is dangerous to any woman."

Soon after his release from prison, Sweeney found another high-paying job as a head chef at a chic restaurant in Santa Monica called "The Chronicle." The new position didn't last long, though - Sweeney was fired after Dunne's family and friends descended on the restaurant with handbills that were distributed to guests and passers-by.

"The hands that prepared your food strangled Dominique Dunne on October 30, 1982," the handbills read.

Sweeney left Los Angeles for Seattle in 1989, and changed his name to John Maura. According to some sources, he is currently employed there as an executive chef for a chain restaurant.

"This guy gets to be reinstated as the head chef in a restaurant as if nothing ever happened," said Dunne's older brother, actor Griffin

Dunne. "If she had lived, she'd be an actress everyone in the world would know... he's a murderer; he's murdered and I think he will do it again."

Another friend of the family echoed these thoughts, adding that "the verdict almost says it's okay to kill the one you love."

THE MURDER OF LANA CLARKSON

NINA LANE

Hollywood is a place where everything is possible. It is a land of dreams and people flock to this city on the west coast in order to find a better life and create a brighter future for them. Unfortunately, Hollywood has its dark and seedy side as well. Starting with the murder of the Black Dahlia, the tabloids couldn't get enough of intriguing stories coming straight from this part of Los Angeles.

Just like the majority of California girls, Lana Clarkson wanted to become famous. She had that superstar look and when her family moved to Los Angeles, Lana did her best to make a name for herself in the entertainment industry. She had no idea that an accidental encounter with a world famous producer and mad musical genius Phil Spector will be fatal and end her hopes and dreams of international fame. So let's dive a little bit deeper into their lives and everything that preceded this unfortunate event that captured the public's attention in the 2000s.

Early life

Lana Clarkson was born on 5th of April, 1962 in Long Beach, California. She grew up in a large family that included both parents, one brother, and one sister. They were very close because of the small age gap between the siblings. Lana focused on her education and was moderately successful, attending Pacific Union College and she didn't even think about Hollywood fame back in those days. Everything changed for the Clarkson family after the death of their father. They relocated to Los Angeles in hopes of finding better employment opportunities.

Hollywood values youth and beauty so it was clear that Lana will fit right in. Her height and beautiful long blonde hair made her incredibly attractive. Since she was already in Los Angeles, she had a perfect opportunity to try her luck and audition for a couple of movie roles. She was 5"11" which is the perfect height for modeling so Lana made a decision to enter the world of fashion and see how it goes. Lana had the supermodel look and was quickly noticed by modeling agencies. She appeared in numerous spreads but didn't achieve the worldwide fame. However, she made a name for herself in Los Angeles and Lana though it might be the perfect time to launch her movie career.

Breakthrough

The movie industry was blossoming in the 1980s with numerous huge blockbusters getting released every single month. The competition was tough and sometimes all you needed was a bit of luck to get the best role that would launch you to stardom. Since Lana was already a model, she was offered non-speaking roles in the very beginning of her acting career. You could see her in the background of many movies and TV shows of that time. She was stunning and you simply couldn't take your eyes off her.

Her first big acting job was in *Fast Times at Ridgemont High*. It was a small movie at that time but it now has a cult status. Her role wasn't prominent and Lana appeared in just a couple of scenes. But it was enough to get noticed by acclaimed Hollywood producers who are always on a lookout for new stars. She had a couple smaller roles in 1982 but her career was launched once she became Roger Corman's favorite muse.

Roger Corman's movies were aimed at teenagers and often included fantasy characters that relied on their physical appearance. Lana's beauty and height were an ideal combination and Corman decided to give her a supporting role in *Deathstalker*. She played a strong female warrior and it was clear she was perfect for that role. *Barbarian Queen* was her next movie and it was obvious that she found her niche. Corman's movies weren't super successful back in the 1980s, but they did have a large following even then and Lana was a fan favorite. Her body was simply amazing and she looked incredibly good in the costumes. She wasn't shy and often filmed nude scenes.

Lana continued making similar movies all throughout that decade. She did appear in a sequel to *Barbarian Queen*. That movie also included tiny costumes and nudity which were the recurring details in these fantasy flicks.

Lana Clarkson was a humanitarian and would often volunteer for charity organizations. As a matter of fact, Lana was one of the first celebrities who offered her help to those suffering from AIDS and HIV. The disease itself wasn't well researched back then and the public was generally afraid of the virus. Lana didn't care about it and would deliver food to patients in the Los Angeles area.

She made a turn in the 1990s and decided to start accepting horror movie roles. Fantasy and horror would often overlap and her role in *Haunting of Morella* was particularly interesting because she played a lesbian character. Lana continued to model and she would often travel all around the world which did have an impact on her movie career. She didn't get too many roles in the 1990s but continued to make guest appearances on various TV shows.

The movies she made with Corman were still popular and Lana would appear at conventions with rest of the cast. She had a following and they adored her. Lana treated her fans with a lot of respect and she was genuinely happy to sing autographs and speak to them. Unfortunately, her fame started to fade away as Lana got older. After all, the majority of her roles depended on her stunning body and youthful looks. Luckily, Lana accepted the modern technology and she launched her own website for the fans. She would sell merchandise and various autographed items. The pay wasn't enormous but it was enough for her.

Lana planned to reinvent her career in the beginning of 2000. She started taking classes and wanted to land her first comedic role. She opened her own production house called Living Doll Productions and was looking forward to creating and starring in her own movie projects. Unfortunately, she lacked funds and decided to take up some extra work. She became a hostess at the House of Blues. The House of Blues is one of the most popular places on the Sunset Boulevard in the very heart of Los Angeles. Many celebrities party there and it is co-owned by Dan Aykroyd. Phil Spector, who was a famous music producer that revolutionized rock n roll music was a regular guest there.

The infamous producer

Phil Spector was born on 26th of December 1939. After spending his early childhood in Bronx, New York, his family moved to Los Angeles and Phil became interested in making music. He became somewhat famous with this band The Teddy Bears. The duo had a hit song in 1958 but Phil soon came to realize that he had a bad case of stage fright and his performances were influenced greatly by it. Instead of working on getting over that problem, Phil focused on producing and he invented the so-called wall of sound which will make him well-known among musicians.

Over the course of the 1960s, Phil collaborated with numerous stars, bringing a whole new perspective to their music and providing them with fresh and innovative ideas. He was a manager to some of the most well-known bands of the decade such as the Ronettes. Spector worked with the Beatles and was John Lennon's favorite producer. As the years passed by, Spector started to become a recluse, carefully picking out his new projects and musicians to collaborate with. Spector was a short man who would often dress up in unusual clothing and he loved wearing wigs. His recognizable sound wasn't as popular as before during the 1990s but Spector continued to lead a wild life, going out every single night and retreating to his so-called castle in Alhambra which is a suburb of Los Angeles.

The night of Lana's death

Lana Clarkson arrived at her job at the House of Blues on 2nd of February 2003. She was managing the VIP area that night and she was her typical self, treating every guest kindly and with respect. Phil Spector started his night out somewhere around 07:00 PM by taking his first date for a dinner. He would shortly meet his second date for the evening and would eventually ask his driver to go to the House of Blues as their last stop. He was a well-known figure there and even though the place was crowded, he knew that a table was waiting for him inside.

When Spector approached the VIP area, Lana didn't recognize him. As a matter of fact, she told him: "Madam, you are not allowed to enter." Spector was wearing one of his wigs and Lana had mistaken him for a woman. Lana's friend quickly pulled her to the side and explained that the "madam" was actually Phil Spector. The fact that Lana had no idea who he was shouldn't surprise anyone because, by that time, Spector wasn't a household name. She apologized to him and found Spector a table to sit at. She was a wonderful hostess and Spector noticed it right away. He was blown away by her height and beauty.

Lana's shift ended sometime before two AM and she packed things in order to go home and rest for the night. She exited the House of Blues and went to get her car. The surveillance from the House of Blues would later reveal that Lana was approached by Spector's car as she was leaving at half past two. You can clearly see that she entered the vehicle and drove away with him. Spector invited Lana to his castle in order to have a drink. Lana probably accepted the invitation out of politeness because she learned that Spector was a big name and she didn't want to insult him. Plus, networking is incredibly important in Hollywood.

It is unclear when they arrived at Spector's house but Adriano de Souza, the driver of the car remained parked in front of the mansion. Spector exited the house in the early hours, stood in front of the car with a gun in his hand and said to de Souza: "I think I've killed someone." De Souza was speechless at the moment but he knew he had to call the police. He did hear a loud sound before Spector appeared in front of him but had no idea what happened inside of the house. The driver entered the mansion, found the phone and talked to the 911 operator for a couple of minutes. The police were quickly dispatched to Alhambra and they arrived at the crime scene. They were met by a grisly scene right there in the foyer of the house.

The analysis of the crime scene

When the police showed up at the Spector's house at 05:10 AM, they found Lana's body in a chair near the main entrance. She was slumped back and had a visible gunshot wound in her mouth. Spector who remained in the house was frantic and the detectives noticed that he was intoxicated. The arrest was made immediately and Spector was transported to the police station in order to be interrogated. The remaining police officers continued to investigate the crime scene in order to put the pieces back together and find out what happened in those early morning hours prior to the murder.

The gun was laying on the floor near Lana's body. It was wiped clean and had no fingerprints on it which was very strange, especially since Spector claimed that the shooting was an accident and that Lana decided to take her own life. The police officers were unsure about whose weapon it was. They quickly found a cabinet drawer that was partially open. It contained an empty gun holster that matched the weapon find by Lana's body so it was obvious that the gun belonged to Spector. As a matter of fact, they would later uncover nine more firearms all around the house which indicated that Spector was an avid gun collector.

Back at the station, Spector told the investigators that Lana committed suicide. That story was flawed from the very beginning, especially because the police officers knew that Spector told his driver that he had murdered Lana. The suicide theory was very unlikely and Spector refused to continue talking to them without his lawyer present in the interrogation room.

The detectives were combing through the house and they found proof that Spector tried to clean up the murder scene. A bloody cloth was discovered in a nearby bathroom while Lana's blood was found all around the house. Spector's hands were bloody and he left the marks on door handles and the staircase leading to his bedroom. Investigators followed the trail and discovered Spector's coat hanging in his closet. It had blood speckles on it. They would later confirm that Spector wore it on the night out and was likely in the same coat when he murdered Lana. They collected the clothes and sent everything for blood spatter analysis. It will become one of the main evidence in this case.

Phil Spector was charged with the murder of Lana Clarkson and the bail was set for one million dollars. Spector was shortly released because he had the money and the power. He didn't return to the house right away since it was still investigated by the police. Instead, he hid in a hotel for a week until he got the approval from the authorities. The suicide theory wasn't completely ruled out yet and the police had to investigate every single possible aspect of the story.

Lana's career wasn't going too well at the moment and was stalled due to the accident she had in 2001 when she broke both of her wrists. Her friends did report that she was feeling a bit down back then. However, she recovered and seemed perfectly healthy and happy at the time of the murder. She had no good reason to kill herself that night. Spector would continue talking to the media and friends about his innocence and would mention the suicide theory to everyone. He was heard saying that Lana "kissed the gun" that night which was an appalling quote by someone who was a suspect in this murder. It proved how inconsiderate he was to the family and friends of Lana Clarkson.

It took seven months for the police to completely rule out the possibility of suicide. After a thorough examination of the crime scene and all the evidence, the coroner confirmed that Lana's death was a homicide. Dr. Louis Pena examined Lana's body and came to a conclusion that a bullet cut off her spine through the mouth, leading to the instant death. He would later say that it was difficult to determine whether it was a suicide or a homicide with that fact only but he did take other evidence into the consideration. The crime scene indicated that the death of Lana Clarkson was a homicide and Dr. Pena stood firmly by his decision during the trial.

Phil Spector was charged with murder in November of 2003, exactly nine months after the event. As it was expected, Spector pleaded not guilty and he started getting ready for the big trial. He was a wealthy man that could afford the best defense in the country so he had an excellent team of lawyers behind him. Spector was used to getting what he wanted and he was sure that he couldn't lose in court.

The trial

In the years prior to the trial, Phil Spector made a couple of videos which were uploaded to his official website. They show a hectic Spector trying to defend himself by stating he had no real motive for the murder and continued saying that Lana Clarkson decided to commit suicide that night at his house. He didn't give any good explanation to the fact that Lana apparently found his own gun in a drawer. The videos also show Spector strolling through his home and playing music. They are a rare insight into the odd life of Phil Spector but the clips didn't persuade the public to change their minds.

One of the most memorable quotes from these videos is a segment in which Spector openly defends himself. He said: "I did not have anything to do with her death. She may have accidently taken her own life. She may have purposely taken her own life. She may have been eating the gun while dancing. She may have been doing anything. I don't know why, when, how, or where and in what circumstances she may have taken her own life. Whether she planned to or not." It was clear from Spector's tone of voice and the way he was speaking in these videos that he was doing everything in order to prove his version of the story. But they also indicated that he was mentally unstable.

The trial was just around the corner and Spector started selecting his lawyers. Robert Shapiro, a well-known Hollywood attorney who became famous because he was a part of O.J. Simpson's dream team represented Spector during pretrial hearings but he was soon replaced by Bruce Cutler before the actual trial. Bruce Cutler wasn't an unknown. As a matter of fact, he had close ties to the Gotti family and was John Gotti's lawyer for years. The trial began in March of 2007 and the courtroom was filled with the media. Everything was televised and Spector showed his odd sense of style by wearing outrageous wigs and clothes. He was putting on a show and the public was more focused on the way he looked than the trial itself.

Alan Jackson was leading the prosecution and he was set on bringing justice to Lana and her family. He was aware of the fact that the famous people know their way around justice but he did his best to present this case to the jury and put Spector behind the bars for good. They explored Spector's past to the smallest details and managed to find enough evidence to prove that he was known for pulling guns on people who were close to him, especially on his wives, girlfriends, and lovers.

The prosecution focused their efforts on the evidence collected from the crime scene itself and they started putting the pieces back together in order to paint a clear picture for the jury. They combined the gunshot wound with the blood spatter patterns found on Spector's clothes, as well as an odd positioning of the gun which was found next to Lana. She was right handed but the gun was by her left leg which didn't fit with the suicide theory. The blood drops which were discovered on Spector's white suit indicated that he was right in front of her when the gun was discharged.

She was found in an odd pose and it looked like Lana was trying to move away from whoever was holding the gun in her face. The defense stuck to the suicide theory and called Lana's friends and acquaintances to the stand in order to prove that Lana was depressed at the time of the event. They wanted to show the jury that Lana was a failed actress that was in financial problems and that she was very likely suicidal.

The prosecution had five witnesses and each of them was in a relationship with Spector at some point of time. They told similar stories about Spector who used to threaten them with guns and rifles when he was drunk. He didn't hold his alcohol well and would often get violent if a woman tried to leave. If we take into the consideration that Lana Clarkson had her coat on and the purse was hanging from her shoulder when she was found by the investigators, it looks like the similar thing happened here as well. Unfortunately, the end result was deadly. Spector obviously has a pattern of behavior with women. He has to be in control at all times and threatening someone with a firearm is an effective way to keep them in place.

The trial turned out to be longer than expected, mostly because Spector didn't show any respect to the prosecution and the judge. He switched lawyers at the last moment, firing Bruce Cutler in August of 2007. Linda Kenney Baden became the lead defense lawyer. After each side delivered their final words, the jury retreated in order to deliberate on the final verdict. The prosecution was certain they had a solid case against Spector and that nothing could go wrong. They had the physical evidence, the witnesses, and Spector's strange behavior.

The jury deliberated for twelve days which was a shock to nearly everyone. It was obvious that some members were unsure about the decision so the outcome was a mystery to everyone. They couldn't reach a final conclusion because two jury members simply couldn't be swayed. The result was a hung jury which resulted in the mistrial. The prosecution was shocked but they were more determined than ever to bring Spector to justice. The infamous myth that famous people have a free pass for nearly everything had to be shattered.

The second trial

The prosecution had to move fast and Alan Jackson remained at his position of the head prosecutor. He knew that they had a clear case but they wanted to make sure every single member of the new jury got the evidence right. They quickly filed the papers for the next trial and it was set to begin in October of 2008, a little bit over one year after the mistrial. The same judge was assigned for the second trial as well.

While the defense stuck to their previous tactic in claiming that Lana Clarkson committed suicide in Spector's mansion, the prosecution's goal was to present the evidence as clearly as possible in order to remove any traces of doubt from the jury. Doron Weinberg who was in the defense team asked Spector to tone down his appearance a little bit and avoid changing his hairstyle so often. They tried to make the jury feel sympathetic towards him. The judge banned cameras from the courtroom and the trial wasn't televised.

Spector appeared in front of the jury on 26th of March, 2009 and the case was presented to the selected twelve members. The hearings lasted for nineteen days and they reached the verdict pretty quickly. Only two jurors were in favor of Spector's innocence and they examined each and every testimony closely in order to reach the unanimous verdict. It appears that the jury in the second trial understood the evidence properly and the final decision was made.

Phil Spector was found guilty of murder 13th of April, 2009. An additional sentencing for using a firearm was included. The sentence was nineteen years to life with the possibility of the parole and it was delivered to him in May of the same year. He is currently being held in California Health Care Facility which is a part of California State Prison in Stockton.

Appeals and the aftermath

Spector's attorneys filed for a review of the sentencing in May 2011 but their request was denied. They made a second attempt in December of the same year in front of Supreme Court of the United States stating their defendant's rights were violated. Their story was that judge was openly on the prosecution's side and providing inappropriate comments about the evidence that led to the guilty verdict. The Supreme Court of the United States dismissed the claims after a close examination of the tapes from the trial itself. Everything was recorded and they found no evidence to support these claims.

They repeated the same petition in 2012 but this time it was in Federal District Court. The judges once again took the case seriously. Their review lasted for three years. Even though Spector's lawyers did their best in order to speed up the process, the investigation was thorough and the case was once again dismissed.

Phil Spector is still behind the bars and he won't be eligible for the parole until 2027. He is currently 77 years old and the chances that he would be set free anytime soon are minimal. This particular case had a huge impact on Hollywood as a community. It was a proof that no matter how rich and famous you are, escaping justice is simply impossible. Yes, the trial lasted for years but Lana Clarkson's family and friends can be sure that the right person was held accountable for this heinous crime.

THE MURDER OF KARYN KUPCINET

64

OLIVIA WATSON

Chapter 1

In the latter half of 1963, Karyn Kupcinet was living in Hollywood while pursuing her one true dream: to become a famous starlet. She was constantly on the lookout for the role that would land her her big break. From an outsider's perspective, Kupcinet was well-equipped for and well on her way to stardom. Her life had all the ingredients: she had a wealthy, well-known father, an actor boyfriend whose career was gaining steam, and dark sultry looks that many would have died for. However, behind the scenes, not all was as it seemed.

In reality, Kupcinet's life was on a dramatic downward spiral in the latter half of 1963. Her relationship with her boyfriend, Andrew Prine, was strained at best and her mental health was deteriorating since undergoing an illegal abortion in July of that year. On November 28, 1963, she was dead.

Karyn Kupcinet's life began in a much-less dramatic manner than in which it was taken though. Karyn Kupcinet was born on March 6, 1941 in Chicago. As a young child, she acquired the nickname "Cookie." That was what her parents liked to call her, so was so sweet she'd give you a toothache.

Karyn did not get her sweet side from her mother though. Esther Kupcinet was often described as not caring about anyone unless they were famous. It was no surprise when she began grooming her young daughter to become an actress. She was from the Gold Coast in Chicago, a picturesque neighborhood that's home to Chicago's most affluent residents. Esther herself was a failed wannabe-dancer who imparted a love of the fame-filled lifestyle into her young daughter.

Her mother, Esther Kupcinet, would be the one to encourage Karyn to pursue acting as a career later in her life, but it would be her father who gave her the means to do so. Karyn's father was Irv Kupcinet, was a well-known and well-respected newspaper columnist for the *Chicago Sun-Times* who also worked as a television talk-show host and radio personality. To many in Chicago, he was known simply, but immediately, as "Kup."

Earlier in his life, Kupcinet was a Philadelphia Eagle. Kupcinet joined the NFL team after playing for the University of North Dakota. He was signed in 1935, and many thought he had a long career ahead of him playing for the team. Unfortunately, after playing only part of his first season, Kupcinet sustained a serious shoulder injury which benched him for the remainder of the season. After surgery Kupcinet was told that his shoulder would never fully recover, so Irv retired from his short run in the NFL.

After retiring from the NFL, Irv Kupcinet decided to combine his love and knowledge of sports with another passion of his that he developed in high school—reporting. Kupcinet took a job as a sports writer for the *Chicago Daily Times*. Kupcinet flourished at the job, and soon began writing about more than just sports. In 1948, Kupcinet was given his own column, *Kup's Column*, which chronicled the nightlife and celebrity scene of Chicago.

Kupcinet's success with the *Chicago Daily Times* filtered through many aspects of his career. The paper had built up his fame, and Kupcinet was now well-known in Chicago. In 1952, Kupcinet translated his fame for television when he landed his own talk show. Later, he was part of a group of talented talk show hosts who replaced Steve Allen on *The Tonight Show*.

By the time Kupcinet launched his talk show in 1952, he was almost a household name in Chicago. Thirty-four years and 15 Emmy Awards later, Kupcinet was a household name across America.

In 1957, Irv's daughter, Karyn Kupcinet, was in high school. She was 16 years old and starting to think about her future for the first time. She knew she wanted to be in the spotlight, she was a natural beauty and she admired her father's fame. Her mother suggested she pursue acting and Karyn loved the idea. She had participated in school plays since she was thirteen but had never thought of pursuing acting as a career before. Karyn soon discovered that having a father with his own television show syndicated on over 70 stations across America opened a lot of doors in Hollywood.

Chapter 2

During high school, Karyn Kupcinet decided she wanted to become a famous actress. She spent her senior year applying to arts colleges across the country and was accepted to Pine Manor College. After graduation, Kupcinet left her hometown and family for Boston, determined to hone her acting skills at the liberal arts college.

Kupcinet's time at Pine Manor was short-lived though. In fact, the young starlet-to-be studied in Boston for only a single semester before packing back up and moving to New York City. In New York, Kupcinet began studying at the Actors Studio, a membership organization for those who are determined to succeed in the world of show business.

Through connections she made at the Actors Studio, and through connections with producers she acquired through her father, Karyn landed her first professional role in the 1961 Jerry Lewis film *The Ladies Man*. In her first role, Kupcinet played a bit part as a young lady in a Hollywood boardinghouse alongside dozens of other young starlet wannabes.

Amongst the crowd of young ladies, Kupcinet managed to stand out. The same year, she appeared in two episodes of *Hawaiian Eye*, an episode of *The Andy Griffith Show*, and an episode of *The Donna Reed Show*.

Kupcinet was getting positive reviews for her roles, and went on to guest star in many other popular television shows. In 1962 she was awarded roles in *The Red Skeleton Show*, and *G.E. True*.

As well as these guest roles, Kupcinet also landed her first starring role in 1962 on the primetime series *Mrs. G. Goes to College*, which was later retitled *The Gertrude Berg Show* for its run. The premise of *The Gertrude Berg Show* was that a middle-aged Jewish widow enrolls in a college as a freshman after her children are all grown up. While at college, she interacts with a variety of younger students and her Cambridge University exchange professor, who was played by Cedric Hardwicke.

Kupcinet played the role of Carol, a classmate of Mrs. G. who dated her good friend Joe Caldwell, who was played by Skip Ward. Kupcinet's character had little dialogue, but her dark, sultry looks stood out from the background.

In 1962, Kupcinet also completed one of her first interviews as an actress on the rise. She was interviewed by the *Los Angeles Times* to help promote *Mrs. G. Goes to College*. This interview was supposed to promote her profile as a hirable, talented actress as well, but many instead thought it provided insight into the extreme pressure the young starlet was facing.

During the interview, Kupcinet spoke highly of her cast mates and the show, but had a difficult time talking about her own involvement in the program. When the questions turned to herself, Kupcinet talked exclusively about food and her body weight.

Despite facing an inner pressure, Kupcinet won more acting roles, which she was praised for. After *Mrs. G. Goes to College* finished its short run, Kupcinet appeared in *The Wide Country,* and *Going My Way*. While her role in these shows were short, her work on *The Wide Country* garnered the attention of one person in particular—the show's star Andrew Prine.

Andrew Prine was an actor who came to Hollywood from Florida in 1957 when he first appeared in a single episode of *U.S. Steel Hour*. By 1962, Prine had hit it big. In the same year, Prine was cast in both the Academy Award-nominated film, *The Miracle Worker*, as Helen Keller's older brother, and in the lead role of the NBC series *The Wide Country*.

The Wide Country was an American Western drama about two brothers who worked in the travelling rodeo circuit. The older brother Mitch, played by Earl Holliman, warns his brother about the dangers of following in his own footsteps in the bronco riding world, but Prine's character, Andy, refuses to listen.

In December of 1962, Andrew Prine crossed Karyn Kupcinet's path when she guest starred on *The Wide Country*. On screen, their characters never interacted, but off screen, the pair couldn't keep their eyes, or their hands, off one another.

The two rising stars began dating each other, and on paper they seemed to be a match made in heaven. They were both young, attractive, and chasing stardom. In reality, however, the relationship was very strained.

Once the puppy love phase of their relationship passed, Prine was hesitant to make the relationship exclusive. They were both busy workers with packed schedules and they were young. Prine had just begun to make his mark in Hollywood, and didn't want to settle down or dedicate too much of his time to another person. Most of all, though, Prine was worried that Kupcinet would be a mar on his good reputation.

Although she was receiving good review for her work, Kupcinet was beginning to crumble under the enormous pressure she felt to follow in her father's footsteps of success. Kupcinet began abusing diet pills in 1961. Diet pills in the 1960s were not the same as they are today. Little was known about the properties of many ingredients, so the FDA often approved substances that were not safe for consumption.

One of the most popular diet pills at the time was Obetrol, which was approved by the FDA on January 19, 1960. Obetrol was marketed as a way to lose and control a person's weight. It was a popular drug at the time, and many believed that it was effective in helping them feel more energetic and lose weight quicker, which is not surprising as it was a formulation of three amphetamine mixed salts, including methamphetamine.

Along with her addiction to diet pills, Kupcinet also began abusing prescription drugs in the early 1960s. This combination proved too much for Kupcinet, who began to deteriorate. Despite coming from a wealthy family who were happy to support the young star, Kupcinet began shoplifting from popular stores and was arrested in 1963 for stealing two books, a sweater, and a pair of capris pants. Andrew Prine was mortified by Kupcinet's arrest, worried about how it would reflect on him through their connection.

By August of 1963, Karyn Kupcinet's relationship with Andrew Prine was all but over. In the previous month, Kupcinet underwent an illegal abortion in Tijuana after becoming pregnant with Prine's child. Prine had encouraged Kupcinet to undergo the procedure to protect both of their reputations and because he had no intention of marrying Kupcinet as she had hoped.

After the procedure, Prine declared their relationship over and began dating other women, but Kupcinet wasn't about to let her first love end quite yet.

Chapter 3

By the latter half of 1963, Karyn Kupcinet had lost her touch on reality. Her first love, Andrew Prine, had finally severed all ties to the young starlet due to her addiction to prescription and diet pills, but she wasn't ready to let go. Kupcinet began stalking Prine at his home, and would write about these experiences in her diary.

July 30th read, *Andy with Anna. Me watched from hedge. Awful. Nightmares.*

August 20th followed, *So humiliated by Andy's lack of interest.*

On October 29th she wrote, *Andy acting ugly. Complete indifference. Scene at his house. I'm hysterical.*

While these short messages tell a foreboding tale, the worst entries came from November.

On the 4th, after hiding in Prine's attic, she wrote *Wish I were dead,* and 24 days later on November 28, 1963, she was.

Months before her death, though, Kupcinet put a great deal of effort into making her Prine believe that her life, and his, were in great danger.

Along with stalking Prine and his new girlfriends at his house, Kupcinet began sending letters to Prine. But these were no ordinary letters. Kupcinet would put together threatening and profanity-filled hate mail composed of words cut from magazines. She sent these letters anonymously to Prine, sometimes skipping the post and dropping them off right on his doorstep.

But Prine suspected Kupcinet was behind these letters, so he confronted her. Luckily for her, Kupcinet had thought ahead and composed several similar letters to herself, claiming they had also been anonymously sent to her. She was hoping this would inspire a desire to protect in Prine, but he remained wary of his unstable ex.

Prine always remembered these startling letters. After Kupcinet's death, he had police examine the letters to see if they could determine who had sent them. The answer was no surprise to him. Investigators were able to find Kupcinet's fingerprints all over them, including on the sticky side of the scotch tape used to secure the frightening messages to the paper.

On the night of November 28, 1963, Kupcinet had dinner with her close friends Mark Goddard and his wife Marcia Rogers Goddard at their Beverly Hills House. She was an hour late for dinner, arriving at 7:30p.m. when the dinner had begun at 6:30p.m. The Goddard's later told police that Kupcinet was surprised they had waited for her to eat, and she hardly touched her food throughout the meal.

This was normal for Kupcinet though, who had struggled with body issues and the pressure to stay thin since high school. What wasn't normal, however, was the state Kupcinet was in. Marcia Goddard told authorities that that night Kupcinet acted very strangely during their last meal together. Her lips seemed numb and her voice sounded funny. She moved her head at odd angles and her pupils were incredibly small.

Mark Goddard had confronted Kupcinet about this odd behaviour during the meal, accusing her of being high. Kupcinet immediately began to cry and deny being on any substances and instead blamed her behaviour on the unsubstantiated claim that she had found an abandoned baby on her doorstep earlier that day.

An hour after she arrived, Kupcinet left the Goddard's house in a taxi cab headed home. She promised to call her friends the next day when she was feeling better. After arriving home, she was visited by two friends of hers, Edward Rubin and Robert Hathaway, who also happened to be neighbors and close friends with her ex-boyfriend.

According to Hathaway and Rubin, the three friends watched TV and had coffee with Kupcinet before she fell asleep beside them on the couch. They woke her up and helped her get to her bedroom. After this, the men said they turned the TV off, locked the doors, and left around 11:15p.m.

The men then headed over to Robert Hathaway's house where they were joined by Andrew Prine himself. The three friends chatted and watched TV until 3:00a.m.

The next day, the Goddard's waited for Karyn Kupcinet's call, but it never came. They figured she must have either forgotten or was too embarrassed about her behaviour to check in so they waited a couple of days. They hardly went half a week without hearing from the young woman, so they figured she would call soon enough.

On the third day with no call, the Goddard's began to panic, so they decided to visit Kupcinet's West Hollywood apartment to make sure she was okay. What they found shocked them both, and would forever remain in their memories.

Chapter 4

November 30, 1963. West Hollywood. It's been three days since Mark and Marcia sent Karyn Kupcinet home from their dinner party after her strange behaviour. That night, Kupcinet had promised to call the couple the next morning to check in, but she never did. Mark now feared that his good friend had died from a drug overdose.

The couple arrived at Kupcinet's West Hollywood apartment around noon. They walked through the unlocked front door and found a horrific sight—Karyn Kupcinet was lying face-down on the couch. She was completely nude.

The Goddard's immediately contacted the police, who began investigating immediately. Initially, it looked like the Goddard's suspicions had been true, that Kupcinet had overdosed on the number of drugs she had been abusing over the course of the last few years. Investigators found prescriptions and numerous bottles of Desoxyn, Miltown, Amvicel, Thyroid extract and Modaline strewn around Kupcinet's bathroom.

There was other evidence in the apartment that Kupcinet may have taken her own life; the strongest piece of evidence they found to support this was a cryptic note found in her bedroom which reflected her emotions regarding her life, her parents, her self-image, and her boyfriend.

This note was written in a haphazard fashion, a similar style to her diary entries. One of the most poignant pieces of the note read:

I'm no good. I'm not really that pretty. My figure's fat and will never be the way my mother wants it. Why must I be so alone. What's the use of living with nothing to believe it?

Clearly, Kupcinet was not in a good mental state in the months leading up to her death, and this note proved that without a doubt.

Also at the scene, investigators realized that Kupcinet had not died that day. In fact, she had been dead for several days. Her body had begun decomposing and there was evidence that flies had found Kupcinet first, laying eggs in her scalp. None of the eggs had hatched yet.

Additionally, there was some evidence of distress around Kupcinet's living room. The TV was on, but the volume was turned almost all the way down. Nearby the couch was a metal coffee pot and a brandy glass full of cigarette butts that had been overturned on the floor. A coffee cup sat on a side table across a room next to a pile of matches that had been shredded and cut up by scissors.

In Kupcinet's bedroom, investigators found that all of her dresser drawers were opened and most of the contents had been flung across the room.

Because it was clear that Kupcinet's mental health was unstable leading up to her death, police weren't sure if the mess they found in the apartment was a sign that a struggle had occurred or simply another indication of Kupcinet's mental distress. Form the scene alone, they were unable to determine whether Kupcinet had died from an attack, an accident, or an unintentional suicide.

Kupcinet's body was transferred to a nearby coroner. Sidney Korshak, a Los Angeles based lawyer that had been friends with the Kupcinet family for years, officially identified her body the next day. Shortly after Kupcinet was officially identified, an autopsy was performed on her corpse. The results of which shocked everyone in the case.

After the coroner completed the autopsy, it was determined that Karyn Kupcinet had in fact been murdered. According to the coroner, she had been dead for two days, and her cause of death was manual strangulation due to injuries on her neck that included a compression fracture to the left side of her hyoid bone with deep soft tissue hemorrhages in her neck, thyroid gland, and larynx.

After the autopsy, Kupcinet's body was returned to her hometown, Chicago, where she was laid to rest just outside of the city in Skokie, Illinois. While over 500 people attended her funeral, Andrew Prine did not.

After Karyn was laid to rest, the Kupcinet family was ready for investigators to discover who had murdered their beloved daughter so they could begin to heal. They had no idea at the time the media frenzy that would surround their daughter's murder later, or that the mystery of her death would never be officially solved.

Chapter 5

Karyn Kupcinet's death was initially highly publicized in the Los Angeles media, especially when it was discovered that another up-and-coming star was the main suspect—Andrew Prine. The LAPD believed that Prine was one of the only people who would have had a motive to kill Kupcinet. If she died, he would no longer be haunted by his ex-girlfriend who refused to let him forget her. As well, Prine strongly suspected that Kupcinet had been behind the threatening letters that tormented him.

As well, Prine had spoken to Kupcinet over the phone several times the day before she died, arguing, which was overheard by multiple sources. Prine had an airtight alibi for the night that Kupcinet was killed, but his friends, Robert Hathaway and Edward Rubin, had admitted to spending time with Kupcinet the night she was killed. The pair had told police that they left Kupcinet's apartment that night around 11:30p.m., but the only witness who could corroborate this was Andrew Prine himself.

Unfortunately, Prine, Hathaway, and Rubin had all admitted to being in Kupcinet's apartment shortly before her death, police were forced to accredit all physical evidence of them in the apartment to other times. They found no physical evidence that could directly tie either of the three men to Kupcinet at the time of her death.

The LAPD, along with Kupcinet's family, was pretty sure the three men were responsible for Karyn's death, but pretty sure doesn't stand up in a court of law. None of the men ever faced charges in the crime.

With no exciting breaks in the case, Karyn Kupcinet's murder quickly fell out of the newspapers in Los Angeles and out of the minds of its residents. It wasn't until 1967 that Kupcinet's story was thought of by many outside of her own family.

In 1967, Penn Jones Jr., a researcher with a love of conspiracy theories, self-published the book *Forgive My Grief II*, which attempted to present a set of facts as evidence that the JFK assassination hadn't happened the way the media and the government had claimed.

John F. Kennedy was assassinated the day before Kupcinet died. According to Jones, who cited an Associated Press story, an unidentified woman had called her local operator twenty minutes before the assassination of the President, warning of the impending attack. Jones believed that the unidentified woman was Karyn Kupcinet.

Jones cited as proof the fact that the call had come from California, and that Kupcinet's murder could have been connected to her spilling a deadly secret. Karyn, Jones claimed, heard about the assassination from her father, Irv Kupcinet, who allegedly had been told by Jack Ruby, Oswald's killer, whom Irv had met in the 1940s.

Irv Kupcinet continued to deny that he or his daughter had any knowledge of the President's assassination before the rest of America right up until his own death in 2003. Kupcinet wrote about his daughter in *Kup's Column*. In 1992, NBC's *Today Show* ran a segment on mysterious deaths that occurred after JFK's assassination, including Karyn's death. Irv again spoke out against the idea that Karyn had any role in the story surrounding the assassination. He insisted again that both his family and the LAPD knew exactly who had been responsible for her death—Andrew Prine, Robert Hathaway, and Edward Rubin—there just wasn't, nor would there ever be, enough evidence to prove it to a court.

When Irv Kupcinet passed away on November 10, 2003, He was laid to rest next to his daughter and wife, who passed away in 2001. Irv's death marked the end of an era to many Chicagoans, just as it put an end to the investigation into Karyn Kupcinet's death.

In her quest to be seen on every silver screen, Karyn Kupcinet lost sight of herself. Striving to be skinny, the young starlet abused her mind and body excess amounts of prescription and diet pills. When her mind went, so did her chances of finding love and happiness, no matter how hard she tried to maintain it.

Karyn Kupcinet's final appearance on television came a year after her death in 1964. Kupcinet had guest starred on an episode of *Perry Mason*, which had been in post-production at the time of her death and the following year. To many who saw her performance, it seemed the young beauty was just beginning her rise to fame, but she was already gone, taken from the world many years too early.

CHRISTA HELM : THE MURDER OF A HOLLYWOOD STARLET

JESSI DILLARD

Disco's Black Dahlia

"I am in way over my head here," Christa Helm wrote in a postcard to a friend, shortly before her body was found on a street in West Hollywood in 1977, stabbed and bludgeoned to death. "I'm into something I can't get out of."

Tall, blonde, and beautiful, Helm never really made it as an actress – despite leaving her home and a new baby to pursue her career in the movies. However, Helm was touted as the "ultimate party girl," and was a known fixture at parties and bedrooms throughout the Hollywood Hills. Her list of conquests included names like Warren Beatty, Joe Namath, Mick Jagger, and the Shah of Iran – and details of these trysts were recorded in Helm's diary, complete with a rating system to evaluate the bedroom skills of these famous men.

When Helm's body was found, police found the diary missing, as well as the tapes Helm had secretly recorded of her sexual encounters. The suspicion was that Helm had been murdered for what she knew, and may have been extorting the celebrities and politicians that she'd bedded. However, the case has remained unsolved, and to this day, no one really knows what exactly happened to the actress known as Christa Helm.

A troubled past

In November, 1949, Harry and Dolores Wohlfeil welcomed their first of three daughters – Sandra Lynn Wohlfeil, who would grow up to go by the name Christa Helm. Three years after Helm was born, her parents divorced. While Harry went on to remarry and have another two children, Dolores descended into alcoholism and entered into a long series of abusive relationships with a number of violent boyfriends.

According to Helm's daughter Nicole, "many of these guys sexually molested my mother, as well as her younger sisters." Nicole said her grandmother, Dolores, was obviously a "tortured soul" who for many years refused to even recognize that the abuse was taking place. Eventually, Nicole added, Helm and her sisters were saved from the "harrowing home life" they had with Dolores, and went to live with their father and his new wife.

As if her difficult family situation wasn't stressful enough, Helm was plagued by a chronic health condition that usually kept her confined to a bulky, uncomfortable back brace. Nicole said Helm and her two sisters all suffered skeletal problems as a result of Dolores' use of diet pills throughout her life – even during her pregnancies.

Thanks to the brace and the countless sexual abuses she endured, Helm's self-esteem suffered, and by her mid-teens, she was acting out with wild, reckless behaviour. Her rebellious attitude and brash personality attracted her plenty of attention from men, though – as did her honey-brown eyes and beautiful blonde hair.

When she was only 16, Helm fell in love for the first time. Gary Clements was a decade older, and rumored to have connections to the mob in Milwaukee. She got pregnant after only a few weeks, leading to a shotgun wedding in Chicago. However, once Nicole was born, the relationship didn't last – according to Nicole, her father "just vanished one day."

"He kind of disappeared from our lives some time after my christening," she said. "I was told that Mom looked high and low for him and that she couldn't find him. My father never did come back. A few months later, Mom was told by someone that he had died in a motorcycle accident in Florida, but she was never sure if that was true."

From humble beginnings

To make ends meet after her daughter was born, Helm found a job working as a waitress at an Italian restaurant on Milwaukee's East Side. Travato's was reportedly run by the syndicate, but 17-year-old Helm needed a way to bring in samone money to support herself and her child. She quickly befriended another waitress, 23-year-old Diane Mitchell. Mitchell still thinks of Helm with fondness, admitting that she "liked her instantly."

"She was down-to-earth and gregarious, as well as very pretty. You wanted to be around (Helm), you know?" Mitchell recalled. "She did what the rest of us only thought about doing."

The women bonded over motherhood, since Mitchell was, at that time, in the middle of a divorce and raising a daughter of her own. Kellena was approximately the same age as Nicole. According to Mitchell, Helm still talked about Clements all the time, and she believed he was "the love of her life."

But Helm was never without suitors. She started seeing a college student named Rolf Siefert while she was working with Mitchell, but not exclusively – the attention she attracted as a result of her bold personality and gorgeous appearance meant Helm could have virtually any man she wanted.

After a time, Helm and Mitchell decided to get an apartment together, a two-bedroom suite located just a few blocks from the restaurant. Nicole and Kellena were staying with their grandmothers, but Mitchell said they would often have them over on weekends. According to Mitchell, Helm invited other people over on the weekends, too – including people she "barely knew."

"I was concerned and told her that it wasn't safe to invite total strangers over to our place like that, but she would just laugh at me. She said it was fine and that I worried too much," Mitchell said. "Lucky thing, most of the people she befriended were fine. There were a couple of strange guys, but, you know, that was (Helm). She didn't seem to be afraid of very much, if anything."

Mitchell added that during that time, Helm wasn't much of a drinker, but did smoke marijuana on occasion – when it was available. She didn't use any other drugs, Mitchell admitted.

Helm's dreams of Hollywood stardom started when she, Mitchell, and two other waitresses were invited by their boss to attend a show at the Playboy Club in Lake Geneva, Wisconsin. The show featured a performance by Gidget star James Darren, and the girls were lucky enough to meet the handsome singer and actor after the show.

"He sat down with us at our table and we were thrilled," Mitchell remembered. "We decided right then and there that we wanted to be Playboy bunnies."

Mitchell and Helm decided to pursue positions at the Chicago club, which was larger than the Playboy Club in Lake Geneva. After the girls were hired "on the spot," Mitchell said they returned several days later for their "bunny fittings," where they were given a tour of the dorm where they would be living and training in both food and drink service.

However, when they returned, Mitchell said her mother "threw a monkey wrench" into the plan and refused to care for her daughter, Kellena, while Mitchell was away working in Chicago.

"I was devastated, as was (Helm)," Mitchell said. "I told her to go to Chicago without me, but she said she didn't want to go alone, so neither of us ever became Playboy bunnies."

When Helm turned 21, the girls decided to leave their daughters in the care of a friend's mother in Virginia so they could move to New York and pursue modeling careers. According to Mitchell, the girls had "no reservations" about having their children stay with Mrs. Gertrude Baker, who Mitchell said was "very nice."

Helm and Mitchell found themselves a room at the local YWCA and started scouring the newspapers to set up modeling interviews. It was a frustrating process, though, since the girls were quite unprepared – with no portfolios, no experience, and no money to fall back on.

"Every newspaper ad was either for straight porno or lesbian-oriented photo shoots," Mitchell admitted. "It was extremely seedy and we got very discouraged."

Eventually, though, the girls managed to find jobs as waitresses. While working at The Gaslight Club, Helm started to date singer Lesley Gore's fiancé before meeting Buffalo Bills football player Ray

Abbruzzese. After dating Abbruzzese for some time, Helm decided to move in with him – and Mitchell decided to pack up and head back home.

"I got tired of living in New York, so I went back to Vermont, picked up my daughter at Mrs. Baker's house, and returned to Milwaukee," Mitchell said. "(Helm) and I kept in touch, and she told me she had begun taking singing and acting lessons at the Gene Frankel Workshop in Manhattan."

A star in the making

Less than a year later, Helm and Abbruzzese's relationship had come to an end, and in 1971 Helm began to date Stuart Duncan, a wealthy Broadway producer who was apparently the primary heir to the fortune of the Lea & Perrin Worcestershire Sauce company.

Helm's modeling career had finally begun to take off, and she began booking regular jobs as a New York fashion model – earning enough to pay for a luxury apartment and even a brand-new Corvette. Duncan persuaded Helm to make a financial investment in his latest stage project, an original, religious musical production that eventually became the show *Godspell*. The production went on to become a huge Broadway hit, netting Helm a sizeable return.

By 1972, Helm was splitting her time between her apartment in the city and a sprawling beachfront home in the beautiful Hamptons of Long Island, where she rubbed shoulders with plenty of celebrities. According to Mitchell, the house was a gift from Duncan, "a token of how much he loved her."

Mitchell recalled visiting Helm at her new house, noting that her long-time friend was finally "living her dream." Helm showed off her recently enlarged breasts and told Mitchell that she was using a new name – acting on the advice of an astrologer. To Mitchell, these were just more examples of Helm's "outrageous" personality.

"I did notice that she had become a bit jaded, but I guess it just went with the territory," Mitchell said, adding that Helm had also started using illegal drugs by this time.

Only 23-years-old, Helm started enhancing her already beautiful appearance with a number of other cosmetic procedures. She also paid to correct her daughter Nicole's eyes – which, according to Mitchell, had been crossed since birth.

Helm wasn't just spending her time with her old friends, though. In New York, she'd made plenty of new acquaintances including Jeremiah Newton, who now works as the Film, Television, and Video Industry Liaison for New York University's Tisch School for the Arts in Manhattan. In the 1970s, though, Newton described himself as a "relentless pub crawler," who frequently visited the Stonewall Inn – a legendary Greenwich Village venue that went on to serve as a landmark for the growing gay pride movement.

Helm was introduced to Newton through their mutual friends Candy Darling and Lennie Barin – both well-known mavericks that freewheeled through New York in the 1970s. Darling, a transsexual friend of Andy Warhol's, lives on in Lou Reed's "Take a Walk on the Wild Side," and Barin was a costume designer who was as known throughout New York City for his flamboyant personality as for his design work.

"Back then, (Helm) was close to both (Barin) and Darling, and while she and I weren't what I would call best friends, she was definitely part of our group," Newton recalled. "I thought that (Helm) was beautiful and an extremely nice person."

Newton remembers Helm's "gorgeous, creamy skin," as well as her beautiful hair and golden skin. He said she'd already had a considerable amount of plastic surgery by that point – including an operation to lengthen her legs, which he said he'd heard had been "quite difficult."

"(Helm) was a straight-shooting, no-nonsense type of person, at least that's how I perceived her to be," Newton added. "She was a fascinating girl."

He also recalled Helm's wealth. When he knew her, he said Helm was living in a seven-room duplex in the East 30s that she called "Merlin's Magical Den." The beautiful apartment was outfitted with an extravagant stereo system, plush white furniture, and an expensive display of crystal figures that Newton remembers quite vividly.

"I was told (Helm) was independently wealthy," Newton said, although a more likely theory is that in those years, Helm received financial support from a number of wealthy male benefactors. "It was understood in our group that she was involved as a major investor in the play *Godspell*, and that she had a lot of money."

Taking the next step

The success of *Godspell*, in fact, encouraged Duncan to pursue production in another medium – film. *Let's Go For Broke* would be Duncan's first independent film, and plans were made to shoot in Haiti in the summer of 1973. The location was selected to help keep the film under budget, but posed considerable additional challenges when it came to creatively addressing government restrictions, and keeping the cast and crew working through frequent, unpleasant bouts of Montezuma's Revenge.

The "high-spirited romp" *Let's Go For Broke* was not only Duncan's first foray into the film industry – it was an opportunity to showcase Helm's talents on the big screen. Helm had previously worked on a horror film in 1972, *The Legacy of Satan*, but it wouldn't be released until 1976. In the meantime, Duncan's newest "spy spoof" was going to make her a star.

Helm, who had dreamed of stardom since childhood, was embracing every bit of her new life as a Hollywood diva. With designers, a make-up artist, and her own hair stylists and colorists,

Helm managed to increase the film's $700,000 budget to well over one million dollars.

Her role in *Let's Go For Broke* was that of "crusading reporter" Jackie Broke – described as "a cross between Barbara Walters and Barbarella," who somehow stumbles upon an international kidnapping conspiracy. Despite many of the other similar films from the early 1970's drawing on the "sexploitation" style, *Let's Go For Broke* maintained a PG rating – Helm refused to do any nude scenes, because she said her family was proud of her.

And not only did Duncan give Helm the opportunity to fill *Let's Go For Broke*'s lead role, he also allowed her to provide the vocals for the title song, which played during the film's credits.

Upon her return to New York, Helm fell back into her old habits – living the life of a disco-dancing party girl. Although she owned a lavish apartment in the city, Helm dated and even moved in with a number of famous suitors including New York Jets football superstar Joe Namath, assistant director Ron Walsh, and adult film producer Joseph (Jonas) Middleton.

With Middleton, Helm co-wrote her first film script – a grind-house film titled Illusions of a Lady that was released in 1974. Helm wasn't credited for her contributions to the project, and she and Middleton split up before the film's North American premiere. According to Helm, Middleton had "insisted" on shooting hardcore scenes for the triple X-rated film, which starred Andrea True and porn legend Jamie Gillis.

"He was shooting it hard," Helm said. "So I got in my car in my bikini and I drove home. He just sat there and let me carry out my own bags. I was livid."

The Hollywood life

Thanks to her popularity in New York, Helm had made a ton of connections in the film industry, and eventually decided to pursue her dream of Hollywood stardom with a move to California. She didn't give up on her party girl ways, though, and continued to hang out with famous musicians, actors, politicians, and even drug dealers.

Almost as soon as she arrived in Hollywood, Helm and her younger sister moved in with Bernard (Bernie) Cornfeld, an internationally renowned financier and insatiable womanizer. Not only did Cornfeld manage his banking, insurance, and mutual funds empire, he also ran a harem in his luxury Beverly Hills mansion. Grayhall Mansion, as it was known, had once belonged to the legendary silent film actor Douglas Fairbanks, Sr., but now housed centerfolds, starlets, and even call girls.

While Helm was certainly no stranger to using her womanly charms to get what she wanted from men and even help further her dream of Hollywood stardom, she was clear about what she would and wouldn't do to get ahead. According to columnist Earl Wilson, Helm had revealed that she'd been offered the chance to become a high-class call girl – but after some thought, Helm had declined the offer. Still, her lifestyle continued to verge on hedonistic.

"She lived as a free agent and frankly enjoyed sex," said a friend of Helm's.

One of Helm's oldest friends, Diane Mitchell, hadn't heard from Helm in over two years. In 1975, Mitchell received a call from her old friend, letting her know that she'd landed a few bit parts in Hollywood and had recently started dating actor Michael Sarrazin.

"It was a short conversation, no more than a few minutes," Mitchell admitted. "I got her telephone number and told her I would call her back. However, when I did call her back some time later, the phone had been disconnected. That was the last time I spoke with (Helm)."

In addition to Sarrazin, Helm continued flirtations with many more famous men – Warren Beatty, George Hamilton, Johnny Rivers, and Desi Arnaz, Jr – during her stay at Cornfeld's. The press also linked her with Englebert Humperdinck, Mick Jagger, and Roman Polansky.

"In the 70s, my mother knew a lot of people in Hollywood," said Helm's daughter, Nicole, who stayed with Helm occasionally in Los Angeles and would sometimes even attend parties with her. In fact, Nicole learned to swim in Humperdinck's famous heart-shaped pool.

"Whenever any male celebrities in town needed an escort, I was told they always thought of Mom first. She seemed to know everyone in town, and was very popular as the girl everyone wanted to be seen with."

Helm had also told friends at the time that she'd even been flown overseas to stay a week with the Shah of Iran. According to Nicole, the rumor was that the United States federal government would use models and starlets to glean information from foreign dignitaries.

"They apparently approached my mother to help them and she began filtering information to them on his activities," Nicole said. "The Shah was said to have given her many beautiful gifts, like jewelry and furs. I was told he was quite smitten with her but, you know, he had lots of other girls like Mom in his harem."

Although Helm was blessed with good looks, ambition, and the popularity to build many connections throughout the film industry, she was struggling to get her acting career off the ground. After her first two years in Los Angeles, she'd only earned herself a handful of gigs – a Coppertone television ad and appearances on two popular television shows. Helm played a roller-skating waitress on an episode of *Starsky and Hutch* in 1976, and for a memorable episode of *Wonder Woman* later that year, she took on a larger role as a beauty pageant contestant with attitude.

Her dream of being a Hollywood movie star still rested on her leading role in *Let's Go For Broke*, but the film production had stalled. Still, Helm continued to promote the film's release every chance she got, and was even rumored to have shot additional (and possibly more explicit) scenes for the now R-rated film.

Faced with life as a struggling actress, Helm decided to take advantage of the singing lessons she'd taken in New York. Thanks to her extensive networking with professionals in the music industry, Helm's desire to release a disco record could easily become a reality. New York DJ Frankie Crocker was brought in by Neil Bogart's Casablanca Records to work with Helm on the album, but Helm butted heads with her new producer.

The project introduced her to her next sexual conquest, though. Helm had begun exploring her "self-professed tendency" to bisexuality, and started seeing one of her backup singers, Patty Collins. Despite the fact that the two were said to be "inseparable," one of Helm's other backup singers, Debbie Danilow, said that Helm came on to her "immediately."

"She let me know she was interested in me (sexually) but wanted me to be comfortable with her first," Danilow said. "I more or less ignored her advances, all the time keeping my eye on Patty – who was keeping her eye on me ... But I accepted (Helm) as she was, and I appreciated her interest in me, even though it was not something we would act upon."

In fact, Danilow had met Helm on the night she was murdered. Although she hadn't gotten much opportunity to get to know Helm, Danilow still described her as "gifted and courageous, brilliant and creative, a rare shining light with no fear."

A night like any other

On February 12, 1977, Helm and her roommate were partying in Hollywood. It was a night like so many others, but would, sadly, come to a tragic and grisly end.

Helm had called a friend, a Hollywood talent scout named Sanford (Sandy) Smith, in an attempt to convince him to come out and join them at the party. When Smith declined, Helm decided to borrow her roommate's car and drive to Smith's house to talk him into it.

According to Smith, he'd been sleeping when she arrived, and he hadn't seen or heard her. It's possible she didn't even make it to the door. It's unclear if Helm was attacked on her way up to Smith's house or on her way back to the car.

Despite being a certified Black Belt, Helm couldn't get out of her assailant's grasp. After she was stabbed more than 30 times, including wounds to her face and neck, she was bludgeoned with a blunt object – possibly the handle of a knife, or maybe even a hammer. Her body was found fairly soon after the attack by a man crossing the street, who apparently discovered her with her roommate's car keys in her hand.

"I was told that my mother was lying partially under a parked car," Nicole said, "and that when he approached her, he heard her let out a long, deep breath – her last."

While Helm had made frequent appearances in the press and in gossip columns, there was surprisingly little coverage about her savage murder. One writer speculated that this may have been due to "who she knew and what she knew." This theory is supported by the fact that Helm's bag was missing – a bag that was thought to contain her "love diary," including valuable information that may have motivated her killer.

According to reports, this journal is said to contain all the names of Helm's famous lovers through the years – accompanied by detailed retellings of their most private moments. Her entanglements varied from industry professionals, actors and musicians, sports stars, and even political figures, like a town mayor who once gifted her with expensive jewelry.

Since Helm's murder more than three decades ago, police have interviewed more than 70 people – evidence collected into four notebooks full of names and pertinent information, and two boxes of investigative notes. DNA has since determined that her killer was a female, and due to the number of vital organs hit during the attack, it's speculated that it could have been the work of a professional contract killer.

The diary, which is said to be "potentially explosive," has never been recovered. Helm was also reported to have kept tapes of her sexual encounters, but these have also never been located. According to some sources, Helm planned to write a tell-all book detailing her history of liaisons with men, and was using the journal and the tapes to collect and preserve information for the book.

Many aspiring Hollywood starlets have fallen prey to the allure of a lifestyle of sex, drugs, money, and fame – but for Helm, this extravagant behaviour came at the ultimate price.

"Her beauty and charm were undeniable, and once she mastered the art of manipulation she found her way onto the path of her dreams," Nicole said. "My mother gained it all, and then lost it all in a very short time."